MW01026474

Beyond Brave

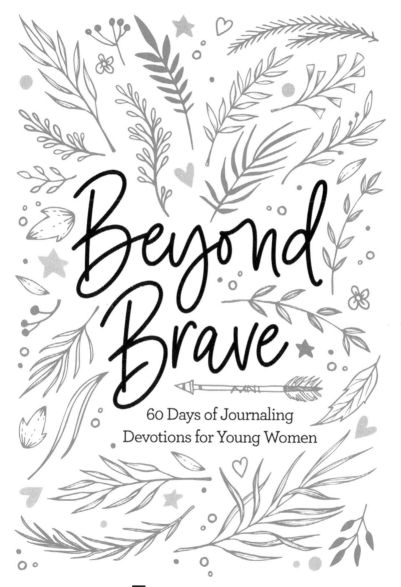

Beyond Brave

60 Days of Journaling
Devotions for Young Women

ZONDERVAN

Beyond Brave
Copyright © 2020 by Zondervan

Requests for information should be addressed to:
Zondervan, *3900 Sparks Dr. SE, Grand Rapids, Michigan 49546*

Print ISBN 978-0-310-76956-9

Ebook ISBN 978-0-310-76957-6

Written by: Estee Zandee
Interior design: Denise Froehlich

Printed in China

19 20 21 22 23 24 / DSC / 10 9 8 7 6 5 4 3 2 1

Contents

Introduction

This world can be a scary and unpredictable place, and, sadly, we rarely get to hear the empowering truth God placed in our souls, or use the courage and strength he's placed in our hearts to thrive no matter what comes our way. But those gifts and promises are definitely there. As we'll discover in the following pages, from the very beginning we were created with a unique calling to be courageous defenders and strong rescuers. God's powerful love emboldens us to become who we were made to be—confident women who protect others, fight for good, speak up for the forgotten, and live lives that are generous and brave—beyond brave. And we have the examples of other women to show us what living in God's love looks like.

Beyond Brave will lead you on an empowering journey through biblical and modern-day stories of heroic women of faith—women who faced the same challenges we face today, and more. We'll learn from their experiences and talk about what it means to grow in our identity as daughters of God, and to overcome fears, face doubt, build strong relationships, help each other, and speak up for ourselves and others. Each day offers a heartening verse to signal the day's theme, an encouraging message, a thoughtful prompt to guide your thoughts, and space to write out your reflections.

This hope-filled, soul-strengthening devotional will inspire you to remember that in this changing world, you have a warrior God who protects and guides you. Through the rich legacy of the women who have gone before us, be inspired to stand strong in who you were made you to be, and ultimately discover the confident strength found in the fierce love of God.

DAY ONE

Warrior

The LORD is a warrior; the
LORD is his name.

EXODUS 15:3

When we think about God, our thoughts usually turn to church, to youth group, or to family prayer time at dinner. We may think of God as our friend or a teacher, or maybe we don't know what to think at all. But we don't usually think of God as a mighty warrior. And we don't often think of how God made women strong warriors too.

This is kind of surprising when you consider how many Bible stories tell of the warriorlike things God has done. At the very beginning, God sparked the universe into existence and continues to uphold it all. In Genesis, God split the Red Sea for the Israelites so they could escape slavery. He routed vast armies and defended the oppressed. Even today, God stands up to bullies and oppressors and protects the vulnerable. But this divine strength and power is perhaps best seen in Jesus. Jesus boldly shared the truth of God's love, fought against those who hurt others, healed the sick and dying, and then painfully gave up his life to save each and every one of us.

Genesis 1 tells us that we are made in God's holy image, reflecting the same strength and bravery. And that means you were made to be a warrior just like our warrior God.

Perhaps *warrior* isn't the first word you would use to describe yourself. Maybe you would choose other words first, like *quiet, funny, nervous, athletic, bored, friendly, tired, kind, anxious,* or *overwhelmed*. But when God looks at you, he sees a beloved daughter. God sees your strong mind, your don't-give-up attitude, and your body, which can learn and do amazing things. God hears your clear voice, sees your excitement and energy, and knows your brave and passionate heart.

Even when you don't feel like a strong and courageous warrior, God wants you to remember how capable you are. You are braver than you realize, and are growing into the powerful woman you were made to be with each day you trust in him. God tells us, "Be strong and courageous. Do not be afraid; do not be discouraged, for the LORD your God will be with you wherever you go" (Joshua 1:9).

How amazing is it that you were made to be strong and bold, *and* that our warrior God will never leave you? No matter what happens or how you feel, God is always with you to help you stand strong.

Journaling Prompt

When was the last time you felt strong, brave, or confident? Maybe it was something you said, something you did, or something you felt. Write that memory down and then ask yourself what the experience revealed about how God made you.

. . . .

. . . .

. . . .

. . . .

. . . .

. . . .

. . . .

. . . .

. . . .

Beyond Brave

....
....
....
....
....
....
....
....
....
....
....
....
....
....
....
....
....
....
....
....
....
....
....
....

DAY TWO

Receiving Love

I have loved you with an everlasting love;
I have drawn you with unfailing kindness.

JEREMIAH 31:3

It takes courage to believe that you are unconditionally loved. That might sound strange at first, but every one of us struggles sometimes with trusting that we are deeply and truly loved by God and those closest to us. The book of Hosea tells the story of a woman who knew this struggle especially well.

Gomer lived in ancient northern Israel. She was known to sleep around, and she jumped from one relationship to the next, always searching for love and validation. We can guess that Gomer had a rough childhood and likely hadn't experienced the kind of faithful love all daughters are made to have. She must have thought love was something she had to work for, something she only got if she gave her body away.

Then a man fell in love with her, and not in the way she was used to. This was real, genuine, love-you-on-your-worst-day kind of love. As you might have guessed, this man was Hosea. And if the sweetness of this romance story wasn't clear enough, his name literally means "salvation." Gomer and Hosea lived happily together for a few years. Gomer had three children—two boys and a baby girl. But even though she finally had the life she'd longed for, Gomer struggled to trust she was really loved. The old lie that she had to work for love came back. So Gomer left Hosea, looking to earn love with someone else.

But real love doesn't give up that easily. God told Hosea, "Go, show your love to your wife again. [. . .] Love her as the Lord loves the Israelites" (Hosea 3:1). Hosea found Gomer and brought her back home, back to her family. There, they renewed their promise to be faithful to each other.

Throughout the centuries, believers have read the story of Gomer and Hosea for the reminder that no matter what useless searching we've done or bad choices we've made, we can always come back home to God's unconditional love.

We're all a little like Gomer, searching for the kind of deep, perfect love that satisfies our hearts. Nothing fills that ache except the always-present, unconditional love of God. But Hosea didn't tell us the end of the story. We don't know if Gomer ever forgot the lie that she had to work for love and chose to trust Hosea's love for her or not. But we do have the same choice. When we decide to believe and trust God's love for us is deep and forever, not a minute goes by when we're not adored by God. Then we are also finally free to stop searching for love, as well as receive that love and start living the brave lives we were made for. What if you chose today to trust God's love for you?

Journaling Prompt

Like Gomer, we all struggle not to believe the lies about love—such as we're only loved if we behave perfectly, get good grades, look pretty, or are the best on the team. What fears do you struggle with? The next time this lie shows up, how can you remember the truth of God's perfect and unconditional love?

....

....

....

Beyond Brave

What God Says About You

*I am pleased with you and
I know you by name.*

EXODUS 33:17

D ay after day, we're told who we are by the world around us. Both consciously and subconsciously, we take in a barrage of messages about who we are or who we should be. We look to culture to tell us if we are beautiful, popular, or successful. We let our school systems tell us if we're smart. We look to our friends and family to tell us that we're likeable, that we belong, and that we're worthy of love.

We humans are made for community, and so this desire to know that we belong, that we're accepted and

Beyond Brave

valued by someone outside of ourselves, is normal and natural. Except that we're not perfect, and our human ideas of what is acceptable and valuable are not perfect. Sadly, in our broken communities, amazing people are pushed out because their lives don't look the way everyone else thinks they should. There's only one voice that's perfect, only one voice that knows you deeply enough to tell you who you are. Let's take a look at the things God says about you.

God knew you before you were born (Jeremiah 1:5).
You were designed and made in God's image
  (Genesis 1:27).
You are deeply known by God (Isaiah 43:1).
You are profoundly loved (Jeremiah 31:3).
You are wonderful (Psalm 139:14) and good (Genesis
  1:31).
You are beautiful (Psalm 45:11).
You are gifted (1 Peter 4:10).
You are saved (Ephesians 2:8) and forgiven (Psalm
  103:8–12).
You are redeemed (Isaiah 44:22).
You are chosen (John 15:16).
You have a purpose (Acts 26:16 and Matthew 28:19).
You are highly valuable (Matthew 10:31).
You are God's friend (John 15:14–15).

God thinks about you a lot (Psalm 139:17–18).

You belong in God's family (Romans 8:15–16).

You are never alone because God is always with you (Isaiah 41:10).

No matter what messages you hear or what labels you're given by others, remember that only God can accurately speak to who you really are. And the messages God tells you are really empowering, really beautiful. But because of our human nature and the broken world we live in, it's not easy to put the truths of what God says above what others say. We have to press into the truths God speaks over us and bravely repeat them to our own hearts until we believe them. But when we do, we get out from underneath the limits that the world puts on us and free ourselves to be the wonderful, loved, accepted, and highly valuable women we truly are.

Journaling Prompt

Which one of the truths God says about you surprised you the most? What one means the most to you?

. . . .

. . . .

Beyond Brave

DAY FOUR

Be the First

If God is for us, who can be against us?

ROMANS 8:31

It takes a lot of guts to do something no one else has ever done before. One of the youngest and most courageous examples of this is Ruby Bridges.

Ruby was born in 1954, in a time when, because of racism, schools in the American South accepted students based on the color of their skin. A significant and famous court case, Brown vs. Board of Education, finally ruled that these segregated schools were unjust and unfair. But many people and many schools were angry with the decision— they preferred to keep things the way they were. Due to the new law, whites-only schools had to change, but these schools tried to make it hard for black students to attend by only accepting those who could pass a difficult exam. Six students, including Ruby, passed the test and were enrolled. Unfortunately, things only got harder.

On Ruby's first day of school, a mob gathered outside, throwing things and shouting threats and insults at her and her family. To protect her, Ruby was escorted into her classroom by federal marshals. In spite of her age—she was only six at the time—Ruby was courageous. She marched right up the front steps and into her new school.

It was never easy. Ruby's family faced overwhelming difficulties, and both black and white neighbors and friends offered help and support. Still, every morning for a year, bullies threatened Ruby on her way to school. She had to be taught by herself because none of the white parents wanted their children to sit in the same classroom she did. It was horribly challenging, but eventually the bullies stopped harassing Ruby, and the other students returned to school. Through it all, Ruby was strong, and she accomplished what she set out do: show she was just as smart and as worthy as other children.

Ruby grew up and became an activist for civil rights. She started a foundation to promote the values of tolerance, respect, and appreciation of all differences, and her work has made a big impact in the United States. In interviews today, Ruby shares how God helped her forgive those who threatened and hurt her and her family.

Racism continues to be a prevalent evil in our world today, but strong people like Ruby Bridges inspire and challenge us to move closer toward equality and justice for everyone.

We may not be facing such an extreme situation as Ruby did when she walked up the school steps all by herself that first day, but we all face times when we have to step up and be the one to do what we know is right. You might find yourself the only girl in a group, the only person who believes in God, or the first one to befriend the shy kid at school or stand up for someone who is being bullied. Or maybe you too need to stand up against something that is happening in your community. Whatever you're facing, remember that, just like Ruby, your courageous example can inspire others to do good.

Journaling Prompt

When have you had to stand up and be the first or only one to do something brave? What did that experience show you about your own strength?

....

....

Beyond Brave

DAY FIVE

Perfect Body

*I praise you because I am fearfully
and wonderfully made; your works
are wonderful, I know that full well.*

PSALM 139:14

Have you ever wished your body looked just a little different? Maybe you wished you were taller or shorter, thinner or more muscular. Every day, we see pictures and hear messages about what the world thinks is beautiful. We look at a friend and think if only we had hair like hers, we would be pretty. It takes a certain kind of courage to really love the precise shape and color of our bodies—just as they are.

It's sad, and oddly sort of encouraging, that women all around the world have felt this way for centuries. Gladys

Aylward, who was born 1902, certainly felt this way. She grew up in London during a time when beautiful women were supposedly tall, blonde, and had blue eyes. Gladys, however, had dark eyes, black hair, and was short. Later on, she was given the nickname "the small woman."

As she grew older, Gladys wanted to do something important with her life and felt God calling her to be a missionary overseas. So she applied to the China Inland Mission and was accepted for a three-month preliminary program. But while she was there, the administrators worried Gladys was struggling and wouldn't be able to learn Chinese, and as a result they decided not to offer her the further training she would need to graduate from their program and be sent to Asia. Undeterred, Gladys pulled all her savings together and bought her own expensive ticket to Shanxi Province. It was a difficult and dangerous journey but, eventually, she arrived and joined a missionary friend in the city of Yangcheng.

Together with her friend, Gladys worked at an inn where she told travelers stories about Jesus. It was there that Gladys realized her body was perfect for this job. She was able to talk and share life with her new community in China more easily because her dark hair and eyes, as well as her shorter stature, was familiar and relatable to the people she met. Not only did Gladys learn to value her body, for a short time she also helped Chinese women embrace and love their own beautiful bodies. She traveled from town to town to show how binding women's feet—a painful practice that kept women's feet very tiny, which made them beautiful in that culture—was very dangerous and unhealthy.

Gladys shared the gospel, advocated for better prisoner care, and adopted and cared for orphans in China and Taiwan for thirty-four years until her death. She was respected and loved for risking her life many times—once to stop a prison riot, and another time to lead one hundred orphans over mountains to safety when war broke out. Regardless of what challenges she faced, Gladys found that her body was perfect for all that God had called her to do.

Journaling Prompt

Sometimes the things we don't like about our bodies are actually gifts. How could the parts of your body you wish were different help you be the person God made you to be?

....

....

....

....

Beyond Brave

DAY SIX

Brave Prayer

*Let us then approach God's throne
of grace with confidence, so that we
may receive mercy and find grace
to help us in our time of need.*

HEBREWS 4:16

Perhaps the most frequent opportunity we have to practice being brave is in daily prayer. It's tempting to see prayer as sending a quick message—we close our eyes, maybe fold our hands, and ask for something . . . then we get up and hope it happens. We forget that prayer is one of the most courageous things we ever do.

Just think about it for a minute. God is the most powerful, smartest, biggest force in the cosmos. God is more wonderful and more astounding than we could ever imagine. In fact, whenever someone saw God in the Bible and tried to explain what it was like, they ran out of ways to describe it. There are no words, photographs, artworks, or charts that could properly show just how stunningly awesome God is. Yet, in prayer, we talk one-on-one with God.

Part of us understands this—the part that feels nervous when we pray or that doesn't really know what to say to a power so mysteriously incredible that we can't even see it. How do you start a conversation with a God like that? Bravely.

See, at one point, it was impossible for us to talk to God, let alone be near him. Sin had destroyed this opportunity because sin always separates, always confuses, always drives away. It was our fault that humanity's conversation with God was interrupted by sin, but we couldn't fix it. So with mercy and compassion, God entered our world through Jesus Christ and made a way for us so that we could talk with each other again. The letter to the Hebrews says, "Sisters, since we have confidence to enter the Most Holy Place by the blood of Jesus [. . .] let us draw near to God with a sincere heart and with the full assurance that faith brings" (10:19, 22).

Because of Jesus' sacrifice, now we don't have to be nervous or unsure when we pray because God invites us to be close with him. We also don't have to worry about what words to say or how to say it when we pray. We can tell God exactly what is on our mind because God invites us to draw near with a sincere and honest heart. We can pray with confidence and make our requests with boldness. In Jeremiah 29:12, God says, "Then you will call on me and come and pray to me, and I will listen to you." God really does long to hear your voice—he delights in your prayers. So don't be shy, unsure, or quiet, but instead jump into this divine conversation with confidence knowing that your prayers are welcome, heard, and loved.

Journaling Prompt

Practice what we learned today by writing a letter to God. Be confident and honest, sharing all that's in your mind and on your heart with the God who longs to hear from you.

Beyond Brave

DAY SEVEN

Using Our Gifts

*Each of you should use whatever gift
you have received to serve others.*

1 PETER 4:10

There's a misconception that in order to be brave, we have to do something totally different than what we normally would or learn a completely new skill. But as we've begun to see in these stories of brave women, it's less about becoming someone different and more about leaning into the strengths and talents we already have. Take Harriet Beecher Stowe, for example.

Harriet was born about fifty years before the Civil War. As a teenager, she attended Hartford Female Seminary, a progressive school that provided physical education and mathematic courses, studies that were usually reserved for men at that time. As Harriet studied classic literature and linguistics, she discovered her talent for writing. After she graduated, she joined a literary social group called the Semi-Colon Club.

Harriet and her husband were deeply committed Christians and passionate about ending slavery. They helped along the Underground Railroad, even hiding fugitives in their home as these escaped slaves made their way to freedom in Canada. Harriet talked with African Americans who had suffered bondage, oppression, and attacks from supporters of slavery, and she wanted to help. Her passion grew after the death of her eighteen-month-old baby boy. In church one day, Harriet was inspired to write a novel showing the evil cruelty of slavery. *Uncle Tom's Cabin* was published in book form in 1852 and sold an astounding 300,000 copies in its first year, making it the bestselling book of the entire nineteenth century, excluding the Bible. It sparked debate and inspired readers to take a stand against slavery. Historians credit Harriet's book as a major factor leading to the Civil War.

Harriet went on to write many other books and articles, using her gift for writing to get others to think about important issues of her day, including equality, women's rights, and Christian living. She told her editor, "I feel now that the time is come when even a woman or a child who can speak a word for freedom and humanity is bound to speak. I hope every woman who can write will not be silent."[1]

At first glance, Harriet didn't do anything radical. But combining her education, passion, and beliefs with her gift of writing, what she knew how to do best, she helped transform an entire nation.

Journaling Prompt

How might you use the gifts, talents, and passions you already have to make a difference in your part of the world?

....

....

....

....

....

....

....

....

....

....

Beyond Brave

The Bible

*For the earth will be filled with the
knowledge of the glory of the Lord
as the waters cover the sea.*

HABAKKUK 2:14

The Bible is one of the most influential books in the world. When you thumb through the thousands of pages of your Bible, it can be an intimidating task to understand everything. After all, scholars spend their lives studying and debating this ancient text.

And there's a lot to learn—it's a curated library of sixty-six books written by individuals thousands of years ago, from different eras, cultures, and languages. It's a mosaic of storytelling, poetry, history, political and social commentary, theology, philosophy, life advice, and even jokes. Yes, parts of the Bible are confusing to us modern readers, but here's the thing: the Bible was written to be understood . . . by you.

Each biblical author was divinely inspired to put pen to paper so that we would have an understanding of God and the meaningful, vibrant life God gives. Though our finite human minds cannot completely understand an infinite God, God really does want to be known. All throughout Scripture, God is constantly introduced and reintroduced to humankind. In Psalm 46:10, God says, "Know that I am God," and again in Jeremiah 9:24, "Let the one who boasts boast about this: that they have the understanding to know me, that I am the LORD."

The Bible not only teaches us about God, it teaches us how to cultivate a God-filled life. It tells stories of people who followed, talked with, wrestled with, argued with, and loved God as they sought that life. And we're told about the Son of God, Jesus Christ, the perfect model for what that meaningful, vibrant, God-filled life looks like. The apostle John puts it this way: "I write these things to you who believe in the name of the Son of God so that you may know that you have eternal life" (1 John 5:13).

One of the most beautiful things about the Bible is that scholars can spend lifetimes searching out its mysteries while children can read it and discover amazing truths.

That's because the Holy Spirit works through Scripture to open our hearts to the knowledge of God.

A remarkable gift, the Bible gives us 24/7 access to divine wisdom, comfort when life hurts, challenges to grow our faith, advice to live well, and most importantly, reminders that God is with us right here, right now. We'll find things we don't understand; that's a given. But when we encounter those questions, we can pray for understanding, ask for guidance from those who have studied the Bible—like pastors and other believers—and read books on the subject. When we read the Bible with humility, when we read it slowly and thoughtfully, we can expect to interact with the presence and knowledge of a God who wants to be understood.

Journaling Prompt

When you think about the Bible as a way we get to know our God who loves us and wants to be known by us, how does it change the way you feel and think about it?

. . . .

. . . .

. . . .

. . . .

Beyond Brave

Ask Questions

*Come, see a man who told me everything
I ever did. Could this be the Messiah?*

JOHN 4:29

For centuries, society has told women when and how to speak. And though we have more freedom now than in years past, we can still feel the everyday pressure to keep our thoughts to ourselves.

Sadly, some people think the Bible proves the lie that women should hold back their thoughts and questions. But this isn't true. In fact, the Bible tells of *many* brave women who spoke up even when they were told not to, like the Samaritan woman at the well.

Though we don't know her name, we can tell she didn't feel like she had a voice. She was a Samaritan, a group of people who were considered outsiders at that time. In addition, as a woman in that culture, it was considered bad manners for her to talk to men in public unless they were family members. And she didn't have a husband to represent her opinion on important issues. But even though society didn't give her a voice, this woman was full of questions.

Jesus met her one day while she drew water from the well. He struck up a conversation with her, inviting her to speak her mind. And pretty quickly, she started asking questions. The more Jesus told her, the more she wanted to know, and Jesus listened and took her questions seriously.

The really beautiful thing is that when this woman wrapped her mind around who Jesus really was and the salvation and love he came to give, she couldn't keep it to herself! She had to share the good news with the rest of her town, so she ran back and told all her friends and neighbors, "Come see a man who knew all about the things I did, who knows me inside and out. Do you think this could be the Messiah?" (John 4:29, *The Message*).

So many people from town wanted to hear what Jesus had to say that for two days, Jesus taught them and answered their questions about God. The Bible tells us, "Many of the Samaritan's from that town believed in him because of the woman's testimony" (John 4:39). Because she was bold enough to speak up even when the pressures around her told her to stay quiet, her life and many of the lives around her were saved.

God has given each one of us a voice. Wherever you find yourself—at school, with our families or friends, with our club or team, at Bible study or youth group—remember that your questions are worth asking and your thoughts are worth speaking. And ultimately, as we boldly speak up, we will be able point others to God.

Journaling Prompt

When does it feel difficult for you to speak up, and why do you think you feel this way? The next time you're in that situation, what can you do to remember that God gave you a voice?

Beyond Brave

DAY TEN

Money Smart

*Lazy hands make for poverty, but
diligent hands bring wealth.*

PROVERBS 10:4

Money. It keeps the world turning, doesn't it? So much of what happens, or doesn't happen, in the world can be traced back to a decision about money. Wars break out over negotiations about oil and trade, poverty continues to exist because social systems are designed to reward the rich and keep the poor destitute, and not many governments or companies want to pay the cost of switching to more earth-friendly transportation and manufacturing technologies.

Money keeps our personal worlds turning too. It influences what we wear, where we live, what we eat, what college we choose, what kind of job we get, the lifestyle we live, or how many iced lattes we can buy. It's tempting to depend on money as the source of our happiness, rather than a resource to grow.

In Matthew 25:14–30, Jesus tells his followers a parable of a rich man who went on a journey and entrusted different amounts of his money to three servants. The first two servants invested the funds wisely and doubled their master's investment. But the third servant was passive with the money he was given; he didn't see it as a resource to grow and so buried it in the ground so nothing could happen with it. When the master returned, he praised the first two servants and invited them to partner with him in his business. But the master criticized the third servant for not stewarding the money he was entrusted with.

Just like the servants in Jesus' parable, we all have been entrusted with money. Some of us have larger allowances than others, some of us work jobs with bigger salaries than others. But however much we have, we all are expected to be good stewards of it. We are not called to be lazy or thoughtless with the funds we have; we're called to be smart with it, grow it, and use it for good. Because money multiplies, literally and figuratively. The more you manage your money well, the more you can care for yourself and your needs, the more you are able to give generously to others. 2 Corinthians 9:6, 11 says, "Remember this: Whoever sows sparingly will also reap sparingly, and whoever sows generously will also reap generously. [. . .] You will be enriched in every way so that you can be generous on every occasion, and through us your generosity will result in thanksgiving to God."

Throughout our lives, we all will have different opportunities to earn, invest, and give money. Let's be smart with financial resources so that we can do good and generous things.

Journaling Prompt

Explore how you might be able to manage your money better. Perhaps you might find a creative way to make money, learn how to take care of the money you're making, or use what you have to do something good for someone else.

Beyond Brave

DAY ELEVEN

Stand Up for What's Right

Learn to do right; seek justice.
Defend the oppressed.

ISAIAH 1:17

Sophie Scholl grew up in Nazi Germany during the time Hitler was waging war across Europe, killing and oppressing millions of people. Hitler and his military officials taught a horrid lie that anyone who didn't fit their vison of the ideal human was inferior and didn't deserve the same right to a free and happy life. Tragically, many believed him.

But Sophie, her family, and the friends she made at her university believed God created and deeply loved everyone and that Hitler's war was wrong. She talked with her university friends long into the night about religion, politics, and how they could stand up to Hitler without causing more deaths. These were dangerous conversations to have because the Nazis arrested and killed anyone who disagreed with them. Even though she was young, Sophie knew she had to do something. She had to stand up for what she believed and encourage others to do the same.

So Sophie did what she knew best. With her brother Hans and a few friends, Sophie created a movement called the White Rose, and wrote articles about their ideas and beliefs the group printed in pamphlets. They handed out as many of these free pamphlets as they could to people in the street to encourage them to think for themselves about what was really right and wrong. As Sophie and her brother handed out their sixth pamphlet, Nazi soldiers arrested and imprisoned them. The very next day and without a trial, they were found guilty of treason and condemned to die. A few hours later, just before she was executed, Sophie said, "How can we expect righteousness to prevail when there is hardly anyone willing to give himself up individually to a righteous cause? Such a fine, sunny day, and I have to go, but what does my death matter, if through us, thousands of people are awakened and stirred to action?"[1]

After her death, a copy of the sixth pamphlet was

smuggled out of Germany and shared on the front lines in Europe. Soldiers of the Allied Forces made millions of prints and dropped them from planes over cities and towns so others could read it. The story of the brave students who lost their lives standing up for what is right inspired the soldiers to keep fighting for what they believed and encouraged others to do everything they could to help. About a year and half later, the Allied Forces won.

Though we don't live under Nazi occupation, we still see injustices every day. And like Sophie, we have the skills and God-given calling to stand up for what is right. Every time we see a bully picking on someone else, or hear someone telling lies, or saying something cruel or racist, or notice a system or group of people that oppresses others, we have the opportunity to rise up and fight for what is right.

Journaling Prompt

What injustices have you noticed around you, and what might you be able to do to take a stand and encourage others to do the same?

. . . .

. . . .

. . . .

Beyond Brave

Brave Friendships

*They all joined together constantly in
prayer, along with the women and Mary
the mother of Jesus, and with his brothers.*

ACTS 1:14

Some of the brightest, sweetest moments in our lives are spent with friends. Few things are better than laughing with your friends so hard that your stomach hurts, or sharing something vulnerable and then hearing your friend say, "Me too," or knowing that your friend will listen to you vent without judgment, and that you are a safe place for them as well.

Good friends give us joy, laughter, advice, a sense of belonging, and confidence in our identities. They remind each other of how strong, smart, and capable we are.

Friendships make us brave.

To grow, friendships require bravery.

It takes honesty to tell a friend that something they said hurt you; it takes courage to call a friend out when they're making a bad decision and not living up to the best of who they are. When it feels like you're the only one keeping the relationship alive, it takes endurance and grace to keep trying. And it takes strength to walk with a friend through a tough time.

One of the most beautiful examples of women walking bravely together is found in Mary and her friendships. We often think of Mary as the young girl who said yes to an angel and then laid baby Jesus in a manger. But her story goes on from there, and we see Mary loving, crying, and praying with the other female followers of Jesus. Jesus' death on the cross was the darkest time in the lives of these women and especially Mary, his mother. They had just watched Jesus suffer a painful death. They missed him and didn't know what to do without him. They feared the same people who killed Jesus would come looking for them. But they stood by each other and comforted one another.

Three days later, Jesus rose back to life, and word spread that God had come and brought salvation to everyone. More and more people joined the little band of believers, and Mary and her friends were there to welcome them all, showing them how to care for each other, share with one another, and pray together. And that's how the church grew—through friendship. Jude 1:20–21 says, "But you, dear friends, by building yourselves up in your most holy faith and praying in the Holy Spirit, keep yourselves in God's love."

Sometimes, friendships are natural and seem to take no work at all. But most of the time, strong and healthy relationships are built by bravely putting ourselves out there and showing those we befriend how much we love each other. After all, that's what Jesus, our first and true friend, did for us.

Whether you are fortunate to have wonderful friendships or feel lonely, remember that Jesus is your faithful friend. He never leaves, always listens, always loves, and is there to help you.

Journaling Prompt

How can you be brave in your relationships? Perhaps you need to be honest or vulnerable with your friend, ask for forgiveness, or tell them how much you care about them and invite them to do something fun?

Beyond Brave

Design Your Life

*Therefore, if anyone is in Christ,
the new creation has come: The
old has gone, the new is here!*

2 CORINTHIANS 5:17

Most of us feel tension between the life we're living now and the life we want to live. We hope someday in the future, we'll start being the person we wish we were, and in the meantime, if we're honest, we kind of coast along. We work, study, hustle . . . we do this and that because that's what everyone else is doing. We adopt the behaviors, likes, and preferences of those around us and switch to autopilot.

Along with the stunning gift of life, God has given you a collection of talents and skills—some you may not have even discovered yet. Already, you've received unique opportunities, with more to come in your future. You have a perspective on the world that's all your own; ideas that will pop up in no one else's mind; and inside you is a dynamic interior world of unique emotions, dreams, and expressions.

Everything in your life can be designed—from what you wear to the thoughts you think, from the food you eat to the career you pursue. This is your life. No one gets to live it for you. People will give you both amazing and terrible advice about what your life should look like, but only you can decide what paths to take and actually make things happen. You get to pick what you're into, what music you like, what food you can't get enough of, what words you say. You decide what hobbies you pick up or put down. You create the routines that help you thrive. And if you don't like something, if you want something different, only you can make the change happen.

All these options can feel overwhelming and exciting at the same time. But identifying just one thing you want to change or one thing you want to add to your life will get you started. Designing your life, living the life you really want, doesn't need to feel intimidating. It can be fun and empowering.

Becoming all you were made to be starts now by

making small, daily choices that move you toward fullness and growth. Second Timothy 1:7 reminds us that, "For the Spirit God gave us does not make us timid, but gives us power, love and self-discipline." Power, love, and self-discipline to be all that God has made you to be.

Coasting means hitting default on all of these customizable settings. Autopilot means hitting snooze on your life. To think about it creatively, only you decide the kind of picture your life will show, only you will dictate the story your life will tell. So open your eyes to the one, wonderful life ahead of you and make it a good one.

Journaling Prompt

Describe the person you hope to be in the future. What's one thing about your life now you can change today to help you grow into the person you want to become?

....

....

....

....

....

....

....

Beyond Brave

DAY FOURTEEN

Forgiveness

*For he has rescued us from the dominion
of darkness and brought us into the
kingdom of the Son he loves, in whom we
have redemption, the forgiveness of sins.*

COLOSSIANS 1:13–14

It was 1940, the second year of World War II. The Nazis invaded Holland and set to work arresting Jews and taking them to concentration camps where millions of people were killed. It was one of the darkest times in human history. But even in the dark, a few lights still shone, and one of them was Corrie ten Boom.

Corrie lived with her sister Betsie and their father on a little street with Dutch and Jewish neighbors. When the Nazis invaded their city, Corrie and her family helped their Jewish neighbors escape by hiding them in a secret room built inside their house. They rescued about eight hundred people. But Nazi soldiers found out about their efforts and arrested the ten Booms. Just ten days after their arrest, Corrie's father died. Corrie and Betsie were taken to Ravensbrück, a concentration camp where they were forced to work long, hard days. But even though they were exhausted and often sick, the two sisters led secret worship services and encouraged the other prisoners by reading a Bible they had snuck in. Then one sad day, Betsie died.

Three weeks later, all the other female prisoners in Corrie's group were killed, but Corrie was released because of a paperwork mistake. She went back to her family's house and continued to hide and help those on the run.

After the war, Corrie traveled to nearby countries to speak about God's love for all people and the forgiveness Jesus Christ came to give. After one of her speeches, a man came up to talk with her. He didn't remember her, but she had never forgotten his face: he was one of the guards at Ravensbrück. He stuck out his hand and said, "I have become a Christian. I know that God has forgiven me for the cruel things I did, but I would like to hear it from your lips as well. Will you forgive me?"

She didn't want to forgive him, she didn't want to

touch him—this man who had hurt her sister and so many other people. Her heart felt dark, but she knew God had forgiven her for all her sins, and because of that it didn't matter whether she *felt* like forgiving this man. Corrie asked God to help her forgive the guard, and, very stiffly, she held out her hand and shook his. As she did, God changed her heart so that she felt God's forgiveness for the guard so powerfully that tears came to her eyes. She was able to tell him, "I forgive you, brother, with all my heart!"[1]

It takes strength to forgive others—especially when our hearts are dark and we don't feel like it. But when we bravely choose to forgive those who hurt us, like Corrie, God's forgiveness changes our hearts and lights up the darkest places.

Journaling Prompt

Who in your life do you need to forgive? Who do you need to ask for forgiveness? As you journal today, ask God to change your heart so you are able to bravely give or receive forgiveness.

Beyond Brave

DAY FIFTEEN

Overcome Obstacles

*I can do all this through him
who gives me strength.*

PHILIPPIANS 4:13

By nature, obstacles are challenging to overcome, but especially so when your own body works against you.

Later known as the fastest woman in the world, Wilma Rudolph was born with the odds stacked against her. Her family lived in poverty in the racially segregated southern US during the 1940s. Born two months premature, Wilma was often sick as a child. By the time she was just four years old, she had battled through measles, mumps, chicken pox, pneumonia, scarlet fever, and polio, which drastically weakened her left leg and foot. She had to wear a leg brace all day, and because there was very little medical care available to African Americans in her hometown of Clarksville, TN, Wilma and her mother traveled two hours twice a week to Nashville, where Wilma could receive treatments. With her family's support and help and a strong personal drive to recover, Wilma learned to walk normally without the brace or any extra means of support by age twelve.

As soon as she was able, Wilma started playing basketball and quickly worked her way to be a starter for the team. She set a record for the most points scored in girls' high school basketball during her sophomore year. Her speed on the court earned her an invitation to train at Tennessee State University. At fourteen, Wilma competed in her first major track event. Massively disappointed by her loss, Wilma grew even more determined to push herself to the next level. Her hard work paid off and she qualified for the Olympics at sixteen, making her the youngest member of the US team. And at the Olympic Games, she helped her relay team earn the bronze medal.

A few years later, she set a world record for the 200-meter dash, which stood for eight years. At the 1960 Games, Wilma became the first American woman ever to win three gold medals in a single Olympiad.

Wilma accomplished all this despite facing racial and gender oppression. She ran during a time when women were not supposed to be athletic. Still, she excelled. "I ran and ran and ran every day," Wilma said, "and I acquired this sense of determination, this sense of spirit that I would never, never give up, no matter what else happened."[1]

For her return after the Olympics, Clarksville planned a parade and festivities, but Wilma adamantly insisted that the celebration be open to all races. That event became the first integrated citywide event in Clarksville's history. Retiring at the height of her career, Wilma joined world-famous preacher Billy Graham in his athlete tour to Japan to encourage athletes across the world in their relationship with God. She later became a teacher and track coach for high school students and generously gave her time and energy to help nonprofits, even starting her own foundation, which provided training to young and underprivileged athletes.

No matter what obstacles she faced—whether caring for her own body, pushing herself to athletic excellence, or overcoming racism and poverty in her own town—Wilma always pushed to achieve her best. Today, she is remembered as one of the twentieth century's greatest athletes.

Journaling Prompt

What does doing your best look like with the obstacles that you face? Like Wilma, how might you be able to cultivate a sense of determination?

Beyond Brave

DAY SIXTEEN

Judging Others

*In humility value others above yourselves,
not looking to your own interests but
each of you to the interests of the others.*

PHILIPPIANS 2:3–4

Have you ever felt judged by someone else? Maybe there are times people misunderstand something you say and they make snap judgements about you; or because of your faith, individuals assume you think a certain way about political issues even when you don't; or perhaps because you listen first, others assume you don't have anything to say and they look over you; or maybe you work really hard to dress and look as though you fit in so people *can't* judge you.

No matter where we go or who we meet, the fact is

humans are competitive and constantly comparing each other. It's as though we're all caught in a popularity battle where we cut each other down with our judgments, push each other into categories, slap labels on one another, and try to climb on top of each other so we seem better than others, at least in our own minds. And if we've experienced one side of this popularity battle, we've probably found ourselves on the other side at some point too.

Perhaps you've glanced at how someone was dressed and assigned them a label in your mind; maybe you assumed your funny friend didn't have anything serious to say; or there were times someone made a decision you didn't agree with and you reached a conclusion about them before you heard the full story.

This battle to be better than others is, ultimately, cowardly. There's no bravery in using others to make ourselves feel better.

Many of us have heard verses like Romans 2:1: "You, therefore, have no excuse, you who pass judgment on someone else, for at whatever point you judge another, you are condemning yourself, because you who pass judgment do the same things." We know God hates it when we hurt each other with our snap judgments. But how do we stop the cycle of feeling judged and then judging others in response?

Imagine if in the battle for popularity, instead of trying to stand on top of each other, we stood beside each other. What if we stopped attempting to selfishly cut each other down and instead worked to build others up? What if it didn't matter so much what others thought about us, because we know who we are and that we're loved by God?

Romans 14:13, 19 says, "Therefore let us stop passing judgment on one another. Instead, make up your mind not to put any stumbling block or obstacle in the way of a brother or sister. [. . .] Let us therefore make every effort to do what leads to peace and to mutual edification."

The next time we find ourselves feeling judged or about to judge someone else, let's make the brave choice to lay down our judgments and stand *beside* each other.

Journaling Prompt

Which side of the popularity battle do you find yourself on the most? The next time this happens, how might you trust God's love for you and practice standing beside others?

Beyond Brave

DAY SEVENTEEN

Kindness

*Whoever is kind to the poor lends
to the LORD, and he will reward
them for what they have done.*

PROVERBS 19:17

Have you ever noticed just how much time, energy, and money we spend on accumulating things? Whether it's a new pair of shoes to keep up with the recent fashion trend, a new accessory to put the finishing touch on our bedroom décor, or the newest smart device, we put a lot of value in material possessions. Our culture and economy are built on this material habit. Yet God teaches us a different lifestyle, and shows us what this looks like in the life of Dorcas.

Dorcas lived in a beautiful city named Joppa. As far

as trends went, Joppa was a good place to live, because its famous ports brought in all the latest styles. Dorcas had a good deal of money and so she could have easily spent her time and funds on expensive things. Instead, as a passionate follower of Jesus, she spent her money and her time caring for the widows in her city.

Back then, life was very difficult for widows. They had access to very few jobs and often could not own their own homes. They had to rely on the help of local churches and the generosity of others. Dorcas made it her life's focus to help the widows and the poor, and to do as many good things for others as possible. Instead of buying things for herself, she provided for others' needs. And instead of focusing her time on herself, she made clothes by hand for the widows—cloaks and robes customized for each person. She gave her energy and her love to the unfortunate and needy and unloved.

Her community relied on her kindness. If anyone needed a little help, they knew they could go to Dorcas and she would do whatever she could. So when she became sick and died, everyone was devastated.

Acts 9 tells us that the apostle Peter was visiting a town near Joppa. Word had spread that because of Peter's faith in Jesus, he could heal people. Desperate, Dorcas' friends went to Peter and begged him to come to Joppa to see if he could help. Peter followed them to Dorcas' house, knelt by her bed, and prayed. Miraculously, God gave Dorcas new life. She opened her eyes, and Peter "took her by the hand and helped her to her feet. Then he called for the believers, especially the widows, and presented her to them alive. This became known all over Joppa, and many people believed in the Lord" (verses 41–42).

Dorcas' kindness and her resurrection are reflections of God's generous love for us all. Her story is a reminder for Christians today to let go of our material habits and instead use our own resources to share kindness with a world in need.

Journaling Prompt

Reflect on how much of your own resources are focused on collecting materials or keeping up with trends. How could you use your time, energy, possessions, or funds to show kindness to someone else?

. . . .

. . . .

. . . .

. . . .

. . . .

Beyond Brave

DAY EIGHTEEN

Using Our Words Well

And whatever you do, whether in word or deed, do it all in the name of the Lord Jesus.

COLOSSIANS 3:17

With the internet, social media, and so many different forms of content available to us, it's clear now more than ever that we live in a text-based culture. The words we say, write, and post have great potential to do great or terrible things. Most likely, you've experienced this in your own life. Maybe someone gave you a compliment and it made your day, or a teacher said you had a gift and it inspired you to develop it. Perhaps terrible words have been thrown at you and they continue to echo painfully in your mind. Or maybe you've seen how words have hurt a friend or sibling. Each year, protests, petitions, public speeches, and viral opinions influence cultural behavior and national policies.

With the potential power of our words, we try not to be careless, cruel, or crass with the things we say. But we're called not just to do the bare minimum—we're meant to be mindful of every word we use. Jesus said, "But I tell you that everyone will have to give account on the day of judgment for every empty word they have spoken. For by your words you will be acquitted, and by your words you will be condemned" (Matthew 12:36–37). And Ephesians 4:29 tells us that every word we say should be "helpful for building others up according to their needs, that it may benefit those who listen." Using every word well is so much more than making a mental note not to swear or insult others. Rather than speaking empty words, how can we use our words for good?

For example, in what ways can you bring goodness and helpfulness into your self-talk? So often the words we direct inward are meaner and more unhelpful than anything we would dream of saying to a complete stranger. The verse above says that our words should benefit those who listen, and sometimes the one who is listening is ourself. What if we used words strategically to help ourselves grow?

And let's consider the social media accounts we follow and the posts we publish. How many contain empty words and how many use their influence to share good?

Also, when we talk with others—whether parents, siblings, friends, teammates, or coworkers—how often are the words we say about ourselves, and how often do we look to encourage and help the one we're talking with?

As Christians, we follow Jesus Christ, the Word of God. So in a very special way, each word we say is a reflection of our love for Jesus. This is more challenging than merely avoiding bad or negative words—it is a beautiful and powerful opportunity to bring goodness into every conversation, every text, every word.

Journaling Prompt

Which example (self-talk, social media, conversations) most hit home to you? How can you use words differently to bring more goodness and encouragement into your world?

Beyond Brave

DAY NINETEEN

Enduring Service

*God is not unjust; he will not forget
your work and the love you have
shown him as you have helped his
people and continue to help them.*

HEBREWS 6:10

Today's young women, like you, are some of the most passionate people when it comes to giving and serving others. There are more charities, ministries, non-profits, and missional start-ups than ever before. We get pumped up and excited when we have the chance to help and make a difference. But time goes by and results are slow to appear, or it doesn't look as if we're making any difference at all. We can lose interest, or worse . . . give up.

Mother Teresa was known as one of the most charitable people in the world, but even she almost gave up.

Mother Teresa was born in Albania, and at twelve years old she knew she wanted to be a missionary. At eighteen years old, she joined the Sisters of Loreto in Ireland and became a nun. She learned basic medical practices there so she could help others, and after leaving Ireland became fluent in five languages so she could minister wherever God took her. She mainly worked in Kolkata, India, eventually leaving the Sisters of Loreto so she could live with and serve the poorest of the poor. She took to heart Deuteronomy 15:7–8: "If anyone is poor [. . .] be openhanded and freely lend them whatever they need."

But it was difficult, especially that first year serving on her own. Mother Teresa didn't have much money and found herself without a place to stay at times. She struggled with loneliness and doubt about her calling. She thought about joining her sisters in Loreto again, but she decided to keep at it, writing in her diary, "Of free choice, my God, and out of love for you, I desire to remain."[1] Even when it was hard, she persisted; even when she didn't see how she was making a difference, she kept giving because it wasn't only about making a difference, it was about showing God's love to others. "Intense love does not measure, it just gives," she said. She also said, "We ourselves feel that what we are doing is just a drop in the ocean. But the ocean would be less because of that missing drop."[2]

Over her years of faithful work, Mother Teresa founded the Missionaries of Charity. So many others had joined her that at the time of her death, her ministry included 610 missions in 123 countries. Her legacy continues today as one of the highest examples of generous service to humanity.

The sort of giving that God calls us to takes strength and endurance. It doesn't quit, it doesn't give up when things are hard or when we don't get results. Because real, genuine giving isn't about the results as much as it's about showing God's love to others.

Journaling Prompt

Have you ever grown frustrated with helping or giving to someone else because you didn't see the results you expected? How would focusing on showing God's love, rather than results, change your actions?

. . . .

. . . .

. . . .

. . . .

Beyond Brave

DAY TWENTY

Never Alone

*Even though I walk through the
darkest valley, I will fear no
evil, for you are with me.*

PSALM 23:4

Imagine being lost in a strange city. You're all alone and trying to find your way home, but you're not sure if you're going in the correct direction. Scary, right? Then imagine your best friend is with you. It's not as scary anymore. You put your heads together, and even if you still don't know where to go, you can work together to figure something out. Later on, you'll laugh about what a crazy adventure it was.

It's amazing what the company of one person can do to change our outlook. Humans are some of the most social species on earth—it's how our bodies are wired. If we spend too much time in isolation, we become unhealthy mentally, emotionally, and physically. But we can face almost anything if we know we're not completely alone. And if the presence of one other human makes such a difference to us, how much more does God's constant presence?

That's why so many stories and passages of the Bible remind us of God's omnipresence—his profound ability to be with us everywhere, all the time. We see it in the very first chapter of the Bible when God walked with Adam and Eve in the garden of Eden. Story after story affirms God's tender presence with us. The Psalms echo this too: "God is our refuge and strength, an ever-present help in trouble. Therefore we will not fear, though the earth give way" (Psalm 46:1–2). At his birth, Jesus is given a special name—Immanuel—which literally means "God with us" (Matthew 1:23). And his life, death, and resurrection introduced us to a God who never leaves us. Jesus' last words to his followers were, "And surely I am with you always, to the very end of the age" (Matthew 28:20).

As much as we try to avoid it, there will be times when we feel terribly lonely, misunderstood, and excluded. Sometimes we'll feel afraid. But that's when we need to remember that our all-powerful and always-present God is with us. Even in the darkest places, in the terrifying moments, on the days when it feels like no one gets us or sees us, God is with us. He's closer than we think. "So do not fear, for I am with you; do not be dismayed, for I am your God. I will strengthen you and help you; I will uphold you with my righteous right hand" (Isaiah 41:10). And when we have the powerful and loving company of God, we know we can bravely face whatever may come.

Journaling Prompt

What point in your day is it the most difficult time to remember that God is with you? How could you use one of the verses in today's devotion to remind yourself that you're never alone?

....
....
....
....
....
....
....
....

Beyond Brave

DAY TWENTY-ONE

Hard Truth

*The king stood by the pillar and renewed
the covenant in the presence of the Lord—
to follow the Lord and keep his commands,
statutes and decrees with all his heart
and all his soul. [. . .] Then all the people
pledged themselves to the covenant.*

2 KINGS 23:3

It's easy to tell the truth when the truth is something fun. But sharing a hard truth—like suggesting to your teammate they should practice more, telling a friend they hurt you, or admitting you have concerns about your sister's relationship . . . that's not so fun. Huldah knew what this was like.

Huldah is one of the most fascinating figures in the

Bible, and we find her in 2 Kings 22. She lived in the kingdom of Judah at a time when the people had completely
forgotten about God. They had lost the Torah (the first
five books of our Bible), and so they had no idea about
the life God wanted for them. Still, there were a handful
of people who believed and had passed their faith on to
others. Huldah was one of these. But what's really inter-
esting is that Huldah was a prophet, someone who heard
God's voice and shared it with others. This made her a
spiritual leader in a time and culture where women wer-
en't really allowed to be leaders. But cultural limitations
don't define God and they didn't define Huldah. She kept
on listening and sharing God's truth with others.

A young king came on the scene: King Josiah. He
rebuilt God's temple, which had been neglected. When
they started the repairs, the priest found the Torah and
gave it to King Josiah to read. The king's heart broke
because his people had forgotten God. He became afraid
for what their disobedience meant for their future. So he
sent his secretary to Huldah to ask her if God was angry
with them.

Some leaders would have felt intimidated and only
told the king things he wanted to hear. But not Huldah.
She said, "Tell the man who sent you to me, 'This is what
the LORD says: I am going to bring disaster on this place

and its people. [. . .] Because they have forsaken me and burned incense to other gods and aroused my anger'" (2 Kings 22:15–17). Talk about hard truth. But Huldah had to tell King Josiah that the country's bad decisions had led to painful consequences. She went on to say that because King Josiah had been responsive to God's Word, God would give Israel a little extra time—as long as King Josiah lived. Josiah used that time well, tearing down idols of false gods, rebuilding temples, and renewing the people's commitment to God. If Huldah had softened the truth, she wouldn't have been able to give the king the warning he needed.

The next time you find yourself wondering whether you should share a not-so-easy truth, remember Huldah and how her message helped a king turn an entire country around.

Journaling Prompt

When has someone told you a hard truth? What difference did it make in your life?

....

....

....

Beyond Brave

DAY TWENTY-TWO

Excellence

*Whatever you do, work at it with
all your heart, as working for the
Lord, not for human masters.*

COLOSSIANS 3:23

Katharina von Bora was a woman ahead of her time. She was born in Germany in 1499, a time when the church was rediscovering what it meant to follow Jesus Christ. Like other children from poor families, Katharina was sent to live in a convent at just five years old. She grew up and learned to read and write, and she helped manage all the different projects that occurred at the convent. But as a teenager, she wasn't satisfied with life as a nun. She knew there was more she could do with her life. However, there was a problem: it was illegal for nuns to leave the convent.

Around that time, Martin Luther, a respected monk and theology professor, challenged the church to look more carefully at the Bible and what it really said about following Christ. Katharina wanted to be part of his work, which became known as the Protestant Reformation. She snuck a letter to Luther, asking for his help in leaving the convent. Luther made arrangements for Katharina and several other nuns to make a midnight escape in the back of a fish delivery wagon. After they made it out safely, Luther then helped each woman find a job or a family to live with. But Katharina wasn't content to settle into country life. She wanted to be part of the work God was doing in the church, so she suggested they marry. After some thought, Luther agreed.

Katharina and Luther moved into a large building that was later nicknamed Lutherhaus. There, Katharina took over all the properties, which included a large farm, orchards, multiple gardens, a brewery, a hotel, and what was basically a conference center for the numerous guests who came to learn from Luther. All the operations totaled the size of a medium business, and she ran and grew it successfully. Her house became an intellectual center for the new church movement. In the evenings, she joined

Luther and his guests in discussing the Bible, faith, politics, and shared ideas on how the church could better show God's heart for all believers. She did all this while raising six biological and four orphan children.

No matter what task she had at hand—whether balancing account books or discussing the mysteries of God's love—Katharina strove for excellence. And not only did her marriage set the standard for what it looked like to have an equal partnership, Katharina set a bold example for all women. At a time when females were supposed to be quiet and humble, Katharina continued to grow as a confident, independent, and strong woman. With the great quality she put into her work, she helped reshape and strengthen the global church.

Journaling Prompt

How does Katharina's example inspire you to strive for excellence in your own life?

....

....

....

....

....

Beyond Brave

DAY TWENTY-THREE

Take Up Space

He brought me out into a spacious place;
he rescued me because he delighted in me.

PSALM 18:19

As women, we're innately attuned to how much space we take. The world has given us a habit of measuring ourselves, and we do it so often that most of us don't even notice it anymore. But it's there. It's in the way we speak quietly or struggle to say things in just the right way; it's in the way we tamp down our joy so our laughter is not too loud. It's in the way we sit, legs crossed and shoulders drawn in; and it's in the way we count every calorie so we don't physically take up too much space. Sometimes, even our dreams are pushed into smaller goals as we're told to be realistic or go after the more secure job options.

The world teaches us to be small. But that is not what God teaches.

The God who made us is vast and full and everywhere. Out of that spaciousness, our Creator made room in all that vastness for the universe. God set aside space just for you. We were made with intention, with design, with color and beauty and ridiculous laughter. We were made to be, and that means being made to take up space.

With God, our world doesn't shrink—it expands. Psalm 31:8 says that God sets our feet in spacious places, and Psalm 119:32 says that God broadens our understanding. As we grow in God's presence, our vast Creator enables us to "grasp how wide and long and high and deep is the love of Christ, and to know this love that surpasses knowledge—that [we] may be filled to the measure of all the fullness of God" (Ephesians 3:18–19).

You were given the physical space of your body, the limitless place of your mind and imagination, and the social circle of your friends and family and community—and you have the depth and height of your own soul, which reaches to understand God's immense love. Add to that your ability to influence the space around you—how you can organize it, shape it, change it into a piece of art, and set it into motion with dance.

So as you go about your day, don't let yourself be

limited by yourself, your coworkers, your classmates, those who are close to you, or even yourself. Whether you're stepping onto the practice field, into a meeting, or onto the stage, don't be small.

Go ahead, take up space.

Journaling Prompt

In what ways have you felt like you have had to limit yourself or make yourself small? How might it look for you to take up space in your life today?

Beyond Brave

DAY TWENTY-FOUR

Brave Faith

*Now faith is confidence in what
we hope for and assurance
about what we do not see.*

HEBREWS 11:1

Jochebed was born as a slave in Egypt. Like other Hebrews, she grew up knowing that her ancestors once lived in the farmland of Canaan, but had moved to Egypt generations ago because of a famine. Exodus 2 tells us the Hebrews' numbers grew while in Egypt, and the Egyptians—growing afraid the Hebrews would take over their kingdom—decided to mistreat and enslave them in hopes of weakening the population. Jochebed also learned about her Creator, who had promised the Hebrews they would eventually go back to their homeland.

With each year, the Hebrews suffered horrible oppression, but no matter how much work their masters forced on them, the number of Hebrew people kept growing. In a cruel move, Pharaoh ordered the death of all Hebrew baby boys. He thought that without any young men, the Hebrews wouldn't be able to fight against him.

Jochebed had two young children, Aaron and Miriam, and she was pregnant. We can imagine that she hoped that her third child would be a girl, however she gave birth to a son. Jochebed hid her boy from Pharaoh's soldiers for as long as she could, but when he was three months old, she couldn't keep him safe anymore. She had nothing left to do but to take a risky step of faith. She wove a basket and covered it in waterproof tar, then packed her baby boy into it as safely as possible. As much as she wanted to keep her baby, she knew if she did, the soldiers would discover her child and kill him. So she gave him the best chance she could and sent his basket floating down the nearby Nile River with a prayer that God would protect him.

Jochebed's baby boy floated down the Nile toward the palace, where Pharaoh's daughter noticed and felt compassion for him. She named him Moses and wanted to adopt him, but she needed someone to nurse and care for the boy until he was old enough to live in the palace. Miriam, who had followed her brother's basket, offered her mother as a nurse. Between Pharaoh's daughter and Jochebed, Moses grew up safely.

Faith rarely feels like certainty. It's more like being sure enough that God has everything in hand to take a risky step even if we don't know how it will all work out. Faith is the belief that even if things fall apart, God's beautiful, redemptive plan is still at work.

Jochebed is remembered as a brave woman in Jewish tradition, and she is highly respected in the Bible (Hebrews 11:23) because her strong faith not only saved her son but sparked a greater movement. Years later, Moses grew up to become Israel's greatest leader, who freed all the Hebrews and led them back to their homeland.

Journaling Prompt

Write about a time when you faced a risky step of faith. What does it mean for you to be "sure enough that God has everything in hand"?

Beyond Brave

DAY TWENTY-FIVE

Risky Decisions

*Now then, please swear to me by the LORD
that you will show kindness to my family,
because I have shown kindness to you.*

JOSHUA 2:12

We all face big decisions that change our lives forever. But because we naturally fear change, we tend to shy away from big changes and instead settle for what's safe and common.

Rahab faced a decision like that when two Hebrew spies showed up on her doorstep. Rahab was a prostitute in Jericho sometime in the thirteenth century BC. Historian Josephus tells us that Rahab ran an inn there. With all of her neighbors, Rahab had seen the young Hebrew nation set up camp outside the city and knew an attack was coming. The people of Jericho had heard how the Hebrew God split the Red Sea and defeated the Egyptian army, and how Joshua's army had conquered their way through the land of Canaan.

If anyone else had opened their door to two Hebrew spies, they would have shouted for the city guards. But Rahab recognized she had an important, risky decision to make—one that would change the course of her life forever. She knew Jericho's false, manmade gods couldn't stand a chance against the mighty Hebrew God. So she did a very gutsy thing. She helped the spies and hid them on her roof when the city guards came knocking. That night, she made a bargain with the spies; she would help them escape and get back to their camp, and in exchange, they would protect her family and accept them into their new nation, "for the LORD your God is God in heaven above and on the earth below" (Joshua 2:11).

The spies agreed, and Rahab helped them escape over the city wall. Then she waited. It must have been terrifying for Rahab. Everything she knew was about to change. She would have to find a new home and a new business. She would join a new community, learn a completely different language and culture, and most importantly, she would discover how to worship and pray to the true God. But Rahab knew she couldn't play it safe.

When the Hebrew army attacked Jericho, true to their word, the spies protected Rahab and her family and led them to safety. The Bible praises Rahab for her faith and tells us that she married and had children, and was an ancestor of Jesus. Though it was terrifying, Rahab's big decision to take a risk and follow God not only saved her family, it became the best decision she ever made.

Journaling Prompt

What risky decision are you facing today? Maybe it's reconciling a broken relationship, selecting a college or picking a major, deciding on the career you want to pursue, quitting a bad habit, or finally committing your whole life to God. What would it look like if you didn't play it safe, but rather made this decision as bravely as you can?

Beyond Brave

Face Conflict

*So watch yourselves. "If your brother
or sister sins against you, rebuke them;
and if they repent, forgive them."*

LUKE 17:3

We all face conflict in one form or another—a disagreement with a friend, unfair treatment by a colleague, an unhealthy relationship, or family tensions. It's difficult to know how to stand up for ourselves and others and then address the issue without making it worse. We can learn from activist Rosa Parks, who set out to address one of the most despicable issues in America's history.

"Our mistreatment was just not right, and I was tired of it," Rosa Parks wrote in her book of personal reflections.

She was talking about the widespread racism that resulted in prejudiced Jim Crow laws. Among many things, these laws horribly restricted the freedom and safety of black individuals. For example, black people couldn't eat, sleep, attend school, receive medical help, or go to church in the same places as white people. If they did, they were arrested, beaten, jailed, sometimes even killed. The city buses had separate rows for white and black people, and if too many whites came on board, black people were expected to give up their seats and stand in the back. And sure enough, that's what happened to Rosa on December 1, 1955. The bus driver asked Rosa to stand and give her seat to a white man, but she refused.

She wrote later, "The more we gave in, the worse they treated us. I kept thinking about my mother and my grandparents, and how strong they were. I knew there was a possibility of being mistreated, but an opportunity was being given to me. [. . .] I knew someone had to take the first step. So I made up my mind not to move."[1] Rosa didn't know what would happen. She might have been harmed like others before her. All she knew was that she had to confront a cruel system.

Rosa was arrested and charged with violating local laws, and Rosa responded by formally challenging the legal system that was so blatantly racist toward her people. Her arrest fueled a rising movement that boycotted city buses for 381 days. At last, the US Supreme Court ruled that the city bus segregation was unconstitutional. Activists like Rosa Parks worked tirelessly for years until the Jim Crow laws were removed.

Rosa's example shows us how to deal with immense conflict. She was focused—she knew what was right and what wasn't, and she understood what needed to be changed so that all people would be treated fairly. When she confronted racism and was arrested, Rosa didn't panic. She was confident in herself, empowered by the memories of her strong family, her prayers, and her trust in God. With focus and peaceful confidence, we are able to face conflict of all kinds and help create a better world.

Journaling Prompt

Reflect on a time when you had to confront someone. How does Rosa's example inspire the way you will deal with conflict next time?

....

....

....

....

Beyond Brave

DAY TWENTY-SEVEN

Quality No Matter What

Whatever your hand finds to do,
do it with all your might.

ECCLESIASTES 9:10

It's good and fair to expect appreciation, praise, and thanks for our efforts and service to others. When we help others, work hard on a team, or collaborate on a project, we want to feel as though we're valued. When we don't feel this way—when we don't receive any appreciation—it's all too tempting to give in and give up the quality of our work. Dorothy Johnson Vaughan understood this feeling in more ways than we can begin to imagine.

Dorothy grew up in the early 1900s when racial

segregation was legally enforced by the Jim Crow laws. Throughout her life, she constantly dealt with racism, public insults, and an oppressive national system that limited her life in every way. As a response, Dorothy developed a stubborn strength and a resilient sense of dignity.

Dorothy graduated high school as the class valedictorian. She earned a full-ride scholarship to college and graduated cum laude at nineteen years old with a bachelor's degree in mathematics. Though encouraged by her professors to go on to graduate school, Dorothy took a job as a math teacher to help her family during the Great Depression.

In her early thirties, Dorothy began working as a mathematician and a programmer at Langley Research Center, where she joined a team of African American women who performed complex computations for aeronautical research data, including flight paths and the calculations necessary to launch the satellites. These women were constantly looked over, underappreciated, and mistreated—forced to use separate buildings, bathrooms, and lunchrooms, and always paid less than their white coworkers. Still, Dorothy did her best even in the face of constant insults and mistreatment. She never slacked off, and her example inspired others to have the same sense of pride and dignity in their work.

Her team made significant contributions to every area of research and helped lay the groundwork for NASA's space program. When the team supervisor passed away, Dorothy picked up the slack and led the team with excellence for years without acknowledgement before Langley finally gave her the promotion.

Always on the cutting edge of her field, Dorothy taught herself computer programming at a time when computers were very difficult to use and understand, and passed on that knowledge to other women so they were prepared for the future. She retired after twenty-eight years, leaving behind a stellar career as a female pioneer in her field.

A devoted and active member of the African Methodist Episcopal Church, Dorothy instilled the same self-respect and hard-working values in her six children.

Sadly, Dorothy's excellent work was never fully appreciated during her lifetime. But every time we do our utmost best, whether our work is appreciated and acknowledged or not, we honor Dorothy's grit and exceptional character.

Journaling Prompt

When have you felt underappreciated or tempted to slack off on your quality? How might the way we approach any task, role, or project reveal our sense of personal dignity?

Beyond Brave

Armor of God

*Put on the full armor of God, so
that you can take your stand.*

EPHESIANS 6:11

Be strong in the Lord and in his mighty power" kicks off one of the most practical and encouraging passages in the New Testament. Paul wrote it to the Christians in Ephesus. Life was pretty good for these people; they weren't suffering or under attack, although war was never very far away. But Paul reminds the Ephesians that like soldiers or athletes, they needed to train and prepare themselves in times of peace so that they would be ready when trouble comes. That advice is just as true for us today. Because as the world has shown, challenges and attacks are never far away, so we have to be prepared. We have to be on guard.

Thankfully, we are given a training plan to equip us for the future—the daily practice of putting on the armor of God.

Belt of Truth: This piece of armor represents the fact understanding is the first step in preparation. How can we prepare for future challenges if we don't know what we're facing? Holding on to truth, even when we don't like what it shows us, helps us know what's coming and how to handle it. When we follow Jesus (who called himself the Truth) and pray regularly, he gives us insights about our world and our own hearts.

Breastplate of Righteousness: Essentially, righteousness is holy integrity, the habit of doing what's right all the time. When we practice doing what's right with the little things—taking care of our bodies, working diligently and with excellence, being kind and fair to others—we prepare ourselves to do what's right even when it's painful or really hard.

Shoes of Peace: Just as Jesus and his followers brought peace and healing everywhere they went, we must try to do the same. This means we don't get involved in petty fights or stir up drama and chaos. Instead, we seek peace and reconciliation wherever we go and with whoever we're near.

Shield of Faith: Faith is being sure that God is here with us and that God's beautiful, redemptive plan is at work in and around us. We practice this by choosing every day to put our trust in God so that when we feel overwhelmed, afraid, or attacked, we are still able to trust him by muscle memory.

Helmet of Salvation and Sword of the Spirit: Ephesians 6:17 defines the sword of the Spirit as the Word of God. And both the gift of salvation and the Bible remind us that God is the savior of our souls and our ultimate protector. We never fight against evil or temptations alone. Whenever life gets difficult, we can go to the Bible and find help, comfort, and advice.

As daughters of God, our warrior King, we should practice putting on our armor so that we are able to stand strong no matter what comes.

Journaling Prompt

Which piece of armor means the most to you and why? On the following pages, turn the armor of God into a personal prayer asking for God's truth, righteousness, peace, and faith to grow in your life.

Beyond Brave

DAY TWENTY-NINE

Speak Up for Others

*Speak up for those who cannot
speak for themselves, for the
rights of all who are destitute.*

PROVERBS 31:8–9

It's easier now than ever to speak our minds. Thanks to the constant presence of the internet, social media, and electronic devices, it only takes a minute to cast your vote, add your perspective to political debates, and influence change. But sadly, there are still groups of people who—due to oppression, racism, or poverty—don't have a voice. As Christians, not only are we called to speak up for what's right, we're called to give voice to those the world tries to silence.

Sojourner Truth was originally named Isabella

Baumfree in 1797. She was born a slave and sold away from her family at just nine years old. For decades, she served various owners and suffered horrible abuse, and watched as her loved ones were treated just as cruelly. As far as the world was concerned, Isabella had no rights and no voice at all.

Isabella was promised her freedom in 1826, but her slave owner changed his mind. She escaped to freedom a little while later and found safety in the home of a Christian couple. About a year later, her five-year-old son was sold illegally. With the help of the couple she lived with, Isabella took her son's case to court. After a long legal battle, she became the first black woman to win a court case against a white man.

Isabella became a devout follower of Christ and moved to New York with her children. She told others that God gave her the new name Sojourner Truth, meaning she was to carry the truth wherever she went. After her children were grown, Sojourner told her friends, "The Spirit calls me, and I must go."[1] Sojourner knew what it was like to be ignored, looked over, and left without a voice, so she decided to speak up for those who were pushed into silence. She packed her bags and became a traveling speaker to promote the abolition of slavery and equal rights for African Americans and women. She joined other abolitionists and suffragists fighting for women's right to vote. Her audiences were impressed by her confidence and articulate speeches.

At a time when the public dialogue centered on the rights of white women and black men, Sojourner Truth was a striking figure who spoke up for the voiceless. Not only was it sadly challenging to speak about the rights of black women then, but it was massively difficult to speak about it *as* a black woman. Despite cultural resistance to her message, she remained confident in her identity and in her faith in God.

Sojourner's brave voice made a major impact on our nation's history and helped set the groundwork for the freedoms we now enjoy today. Her life reminds us to look for those who are marginalized and to help their voices be heard.

Journaling Prompt

Write about a time when someone helped your voice be heard. What would it look like for you to do the same for others?

Beyond Brave

DAY THIRTY

Defy the Norm

*Dear friends, do not believe every spirit,
but test the spirits to see whether they
are from God, because many false
prophets have gone out into the world.*

1 JOHN 4:1

Pandita Ramabai was born in India in 1858. Her father was a scholar of the Hindu scriptures and wisdom texts. Revolutionary for his time, her father thought women should be able to learn to read and recite the holy writings, so his wife and two daughters learned how to read Sanskrit.

Pandita's family traveled from temple to temple to pray and worship. They gave all their money to the gods hoping that, as they were promised, they would be rewarded with good fortune. Instead, both her parents and sister died of starvation, and Pandita and her brother were left to beg for food. At one point, the two orphans came to a temple where they discovered a trick the priests used to convince worshipers to give more money. They both lost their faith and settled in Calcutta.

Pandita thought carefully about the world she lived in, and defied cultural expectations if she didn't think they were right or beneficial. She married a man from a different caste and social group, which was considered inappropriate at that time. Her husband died two years later, leaving Pandita and her young daughter as social outcasts. Widows and orphans had no rights and were frequently forced into prostitution, permanent servitude, or homelessness, but Pandita resisted this societal norm by traveling with her daughter to England, where she studied medicine.

In England, Pandita visited a Christian rescue home for women in need. Seeing that ministry at work made a powerful impression on her. After reading about the life of Jesus, she dedicated her life to following him. England introduced Pandita to the numerous Christian denominations, and she believed this caused more disunion than good. She determined, "I shall not bind myself to believe in and accept everything that is taught by the church; before I accept it I must be convinced that it is according to Christ's teaching."[1]

Back in India, Pandita founded Arya Women's Society

to advocate for women's rights, and Sharada Sadan, or House of Learning, to educate young women. As her faith in Christ grew, Pandita also founded two other ministries, which together provided shelter, food, and education to thousands of women. During famine, Pandita took carts to the surrounding villages to rescue thousands of children and destitute women. Fluent in seven languages, she also translated the Bible from the original Greek and Hebrew into her native language of Marathi so her people could understand it.

Pandita was often the first woman to speak before government officials and national counsels. With each opportunity, she boldly addressed the mistreatment of women and challenged rooms of men to accept gender reforms. Moved by her brilliant reasoning and personal experience, many of her suggested reforms were enacted.

Pandita didn't accept things the way they were, but in education, social practices, government policies, and religious assumptions, she always sought truth, righteousness, and justice.

Journaling Prompt

We don't tend to give a lot of thought to cultural, political, religious norms. How can we seek truth and justice and be

Beyond Brave

more thoughtful about the customs we adopt in our own lives without realizing it?

Women of Valor

*Honor her for all that her hands have
done, and let her works bring her praise.*

PROVERBS 31:31

Proverbs 31 is famously understood as a job description for the perfect godly woman. If you haven't heard a talk about it yet, you probably will soon. It's commonly seen as a to-do list for women to follow, with things like getting up before dawn, going to bed after everyone else, and working vigorously all day long. It sounds exhausting to us and makes us feel as though we've already failed at being women. But many Christians today are interpreting this passage wrong.

Somehow, the real, empowering message of Proverbs 31 gets lost between the ancient Hebrew language and our modern English. And it's time to set the record straight.

Proverbs 31 is a poem dedicated to women. It was written in a completely different time and place and culture, and so some of the creative descriptions sound odd to us today. But even still, this poem is an affirmation of womanhood and an inspiring addition to our female heritage.

In Jewish culture, this poem is a blessing. Every week on the Sabbath, husbands and fathers sing this over their wives and daughters, complimenting and thanking them for their hard work and brave character. Proverbs 31 is decidedly not a to-do list; it's a celebration of women.

It kicks off with a salute to "*eshet chayil*," which means "women of valor." Then the poem gives a beautiful tribute to all women who are strong, wise, smart, and kind. It praises the women who get their hands dirty working hard to do what they love and are skilled to do. It uplifts the women who are generous, who see and help the needs of others. She is noble and courageous. She is so confident in God's love and her own abilities that she can laugh at whatever troubles may come in the future. Essentially, this poem tells us that whatever women of valor do, they do it with grit, bravery, and heart.

This should sound familiar to us. We all know wise moms and grandmas who have the perfect piece of advice to help someone. We know female mentors who give kindly to others, who open their homes to friends and families. We know single and married women who are successful in their work and who are generous with those in need. These are the women of valor.

You are a woman of valor. Every time you practice any one of these traits, you are stepping into your God-given role of a brave and confident woman. And it's something to be proud of—it's the stuff that makes poems and songs. Now as you read Proverbs 31, let it remind you of all the amazing women you know and, ultimately, read it as a celebration of who you are as a fellow woman of valor as well.

Journaling Prompt

Read Proverbs 31:10–31 and mark all the verses that remind you of something you do already. Write about the ways you live as a woman of valor already and the women who inspire you.

. . . .

. . . .

. . . .

. . . .

. . . .

. . . .

Beyond Brave

Share Knowledge

Let the message of Christ dwell among you richly as you teach and admonish one another with all wisdom.

COLOSSIANS 3:16

Nobody wants to be a know-it-all, the one who bores everyone else with loads of information. But sharing useful knowledge is a powerful gift, and in some cases a life-changing one. No one knew this better than Priscilla.

Priscilla and her husband, Aquila, were Christian Jews who lived in Italy (see Acts 18). But when the Roman emperor ordered all Jews to leave because of their belief in God, Priscilla and her family moved to Greece. It was difficult leaving everything they knew behind to find a new home. They settled in the town of Corinth and restarted their tent-making business, eventually making new friends. One of the friends they met was the apostle Paul. He was an important missionary, and his letters make up almost half of the New Testament. For a little while, Paul, Priscilla, and Aquila worked together and shared meals together. They talked about Jesus Christ and how they could share the story of God's grace with others. After a time, Paul left to continue his missionary work and Priscilla and Aquila kept working and telling others God's story.

One day, they met a young missionary named Apollos. Like Paul, Apollos taught others about God wherever he went. But he only knew half of the story. He taught people that a savior was coming, but he didn't know that Jesus Christ had already come, died for our sins, and rose again victoriously. Priscilla invited Apollos to their house one night and shared the greatest information he would ever learn. In one conversation, Priscilla taught Apollos that God's grace and forgiveness wasn't coming someday in the future—it was already here, already given freely to everyone who believed. That news changed Apollos' life and all the lives that he would teach in the future.

After their discussion, Priscilla and Aquila sent Apollos to the believers in western Greece, where he helped them share the whole story of God's love with others.

Throughout history there have been times when

women are discouraged from teaching others, and there are still some settings and groups today where our voices and our knowledge are not welcome. Pricilla lived during one of those times and yet she wasn't intimidated. She understood the importance of the information she had and she knew that she could help others by sharing it. Of course, we can't control what others do with the information we give them. Apollos could have ignored Priscilla's teaching or told her he wasn't interested in anything she had to say. But God doesn't tell us to make sure people put our information to use. He only calls us to share what we know with others.

Like Priscilla, let us not be intimidated by the expectations of others but invite people into the knowledge we have so they can grow too.

Journaling Prompt

Write about a time when someone shared helpful knowledge with you. How did that information help you grow as a person? How might you be able to do the same for someone else?

Beyond Brave

DAY THIRTY-THREE

Brave Peace

*Make every effort to live in peace
with everyone and to be holy.*

HEBREWS 12:14

We often assume peace is the lack of confrontation and that peacemakers are individuals who gently coax others to get along. But true, transformative peace is a bold act.

One of the most respected peacemakers in church history is Catherine of Siena, Italy. When she was about seven years old, Catherine had a beautiful vision of Jesus in heaven. That experience inspired her to commit her entire life to God. As a teenager, her family tried to persuade Catherine to marry, as was the medieval Europe custom. But Catherine was determined to remain solely focused on a life of faithful devotion. Her parents eventually relented, and her father set aside a little room in the basement of their house where Catherine could pray and worship in quiet. Fiercely dedicated to her faith, Catherine gave up all forms of comfort—nice clothes, all except the plainest food, and a soft bed, preferring to sleep on a wooden bench instead. She lived in that little room for three years and prayed nonstop until she felt Christ calling her to rejoin society.

In her twenties, Catherine helped care for victims of the Black Plague, which sadly caused the death of her sister and brother, several nieces and nephews, and eighty thousand people in Siena alone. Catherine brought physical and spiritual peace to the sick with her prayers and care.

Then God called Catherine to serve the greater public, which was fractured by wars and violently divisive political tensions. Corruption and struggles for power prevented the Catholic church—the religious leader of Italy—from being the generous, life-giving, and holy organization that it was created to be. Catherine wrote many bold letters to the pope and other religious authorities, urging them to find peace with one another. She even traveled to the pope's palace to meet face to face with the most important person of her day. It was an unheard-of act, and to make it riskier, Catherine challenged the pope to do what was right, to put aside his selfish desires and lead the church the way Christ had taught. Her bold words worked, and the pope immediately set to work making big changes in the Catholic church. But Catherine's work of peace was just beginning. The pope often requested her advice throughout the years. Eventually, she was made the pope's official peacemaker, the only female to hold that role in that era, and she went on multiple missions to negotiate peace between the church and other political parties.

Sadly, Catherine died young at just thirty-three years old due to a long struggle with anorexia. She is honored as a saint by the Holy Catholic Church. The hundreds of thoughtful and insightful letters she wrote and her ability to find peaceful solutions and influence world leaders challenge us to seek true, transformative peace in our world today.

Journaling Prompt

How does Catherine's life challenge your idea of peacemaking? How might God be calling you to bring real peace into your circles of influence?

....

....

Beyond Brave

DAY THIRTY-FOUR

Rescue Others

Defend the weak and the fatherless;
uphold the cause of the poor
and the oppressed. Rescue the
weak and the needy; deliver them
from the hand of the wicked.

PSALM 82:3–4

Harriet Tubman was one of the most courageous women in the nineteenth century. Born into a family of slaves, Harriet watched as her mother fought to keep the family together when slave owners tried to sell the children away. The family shared Bible stories in the evenings, and as Harriet became an adult, her faith in God grew strong.

Like all slaves, Harriet's life was incredibly difficult. Her owners beat and even raped her as a young girl. At age thirteen, one of her owners threw a heavy metal object at another slave but hit Harriet instead. That concussion gave her terrible headaches and seizures for the rest of her life. Harriet's parents were legally free when they turned forty-five years old, but their owners refused to let them go. This, on top of everything else, inspired Harriet to run away. After careful planning and with an astounding amount of resilience, Harriet made her escape. She said later, "There was one of two things I had a right to, liberty or death; if I could not have one, I would have the other."[1]

Harriet's escape was extremely risky. If she'd been caught, she would have been killed. But Harriet pushed on, hiding in secret rooms along the Underground Railroad, running from hunting dogs and slave catchers. She walked miles and miles during the night. And at last, she made it to the free state of Pennsylvania. "When I found I had crossed that line, I looked at my hands to see if I was the same person. There was such a glory over everything [. . .] I felt like I was in Heaven."[2]

Amazingly, Harriet snuck back into the slave states even though there was a bounty on her head, and she began leading groups of other slaves into freedom. She made this trip about thirteen times and rescued between sixty and seventy people. Today, Harriet's courageous legacy continues to inspire millions to help and rescue others.

There are still millions of slaves today—women, children, and men forced to live and work in horrible situations around the world. By volunteering and donating to ministries, and by educating others, we can each do a small part in rescuing them.

And in the spirit of Harriet, we can open our eyes to those around us in need of help. Take a look at the people who live nearby. If you have a friend whose home life isn't peaceful, maybe you can invite them into your home whenever they need a safe place. If you have a family member who is struggling financially or academically, perhaps you can help them earn money or offer to tutor them.

Like Harriet, may all women learn to be courageous in the ways they help others.

Journaling Prompt

Write about a time when someone rescued or helped you. How can you help those in need—whether in your community or in the wider world today?

Beyond Brave

DAY THIRTY-FIVE

Difficult People

If you love those who love you,
what reward will you get?

MATTHEW 5:46

We are all connected to people in some way or another who are difficult, thoughtless, lazy, or plain mean. We can be working hard and feeling confident, and then that one difficult person always throws us off our game. How do we deal with those people while keeping our focus and maintaining a brave attitude?

Abigail not only had to deal with a difficult person, she was married to one. Nabal was a wealthy landowner with a thriving livestock business, but he was "surly and mean in his dealings" (1 Samuel 25:3). Nabal often acted harshly and without thinking, leaving Abigail and his employees to clean up the messes he made.

One day, David and his six hundred men moved into the neighborhood. This was the same David who had killed Goliath as a teenager and who would eventually become king of Israel. At this point in his life, he was the leader of a large band of rebel soldiers. David instructed his men to keep an eye on Nabal's livestock to protect the animals from any raiders and thieves. Nabal had one of his most profitable years, thanks to David's protection.

When it was time for David to leave, he sent ten men to Nabal to ask for any extra food supplies he had on hand as a casual payment for the work they had done. But Nabal acted in his usual proud and mean manner and insulted David's name and reputation. Furious, David gathered four hundred of his men and started marching to attack Nabal's place.

Once Abigail learned what had happened, it would have been understandable for her to crumple into despair. She was caught between two difficult people—an idiot husband who had invited an attack on his family, and David, who was about to respond to one man's insults by killing innocent people. She could have panicked and fled. Instead, she faced down an army.

As fast as she could, Abigail packed all the extra food they had and rushed to meet the soldiers. As soon as she saw David, she gave one of the longest monologues by a woman in the Bible (1 Samuel 25:24–31). She acknowledged the foolish mistake Nabal had made and gave generous gifts of food as a peace offering. She even had the courage to remind David that if he really did follow God as he claimed, he would know that getting back at others is God's business, not ours.

David recognized Abigail's wisdom and praised her for saving many lives that day. Back home, Abigail confronted Nabal about his disastrous mistake, and almost immediately he became sick, dying a few days later.

Abigail didn't let the difficult people in her life undermine her values; instead, she rose above them and was even concerned for others' lives and integrity. A true inspiration, she handled a terrible situation with quick thinking and courage, and challenged others to do the same.

Journaling Prompt

How does Abigail's approach to a terrible situation inspire you? How does today's verse challenge the way you deal with difficult people?

....

....

Beyond Brave

Brave Humility

For the LORD takes delight in his people;
he crowns the humble with victory.

PSALM 149:4

Though it may seem like the opposite, in reality humility is a surprising but significant part of being brave. One of the greatest examples of this is the Olympic gold medalist Betty Cuthbert.

Born in Australia in 1938, Betty was a shy kid around other people. But with her twin sister or, better yet, when she was running, Betty was all energy and excitement. With the encouragement of her coaches, Betty started to compete more seriously and started winning championships when she was thirteen. By fifteen, she broke her first national record. Hesitantly, she tried out for the 1956

Olympics in Melbourne, but also bought a spectator ticket with her life savings because she doubted she would make the Australian team.

No one had ever heard of this scrawny kid from Australia, yet Betty not only made the Olympic team, she broke a world record in the 200 meters and helped her team set two additional records. That year, Betty won an astounding three gold medals. She was nicknamed Australia's Golden Girl and the public fell in love with her humble but earnest personality.

Betty kept racing and setting records until a hamstring injury at the 1960 Olympics caused her to retire. She settled into a quieter life, but then one night Betty heard a voice telling her to run again. Recognizing it as God's voice, she said okay and started training.

It took a lot of work to get back into shape, but she raced again at the 1964 Olympics, where she competed in the newly added 400-meter women's race. She took home her fourth gold medal, making her the only Olympian—male or female—to win gold in all four sprint events.

Five years later, Betty was diagnosed with multiple sclerosis (MS), a debilitating disease that attacks the nervous system and eventually forced her to use a wheelchair. But Betty remained positive. She became an encouraging role model for others who suffered with MS, and she

leveraged her fame and publicity to advocate for medical research. Her strength and joy in the midst of fighting the disease inspired a watching world. She said, "I have never questioned God or asked, 'Why me, Lord?' because I love God so much. I continue to trust him."[1]

In her later years, that shy girl became a passionate and outspoken Christian. She shared God's love with all the people she met. "I know people listen to me because they know what I used to do before—run. If they can pick up some encouragement, it might help them. It helps me too."[2]

Betty didn't grow prideful from her success. She didn't become bitter with her diagnoses. Rather, her brave humility enabled her to be fully present in whatever situation she found herself. Betty's legacy reminds us to do the best we can with whatever battle we face.

Journaling Prompt

When have you thought, "Why me?" about a less-than-ideal situation in your life? What would it look to be humble and brave in the areas of your life that seem unexciting or difficult?

....

....

Beyond Brave

Confident Purpose

*There are different kinds of gifts, but
the same Spirit distributes them. There
are different kinds of service, but the
same Lord. There are different kinds
of working, but in all of them and in
everyone it is the same God at work.*

1 CORINTHIANS 12:4–6

You may not know it, but every time you see a red
Salvation Army bucket, you're witnessing the work
of a woman confident in her purpose. But Catherine Booth
wasn't always so confident.

As a young woman, Catherine developed painful spinal
issues that caused her to stay in bed for months. She read a
lot, especially books about theology and the Christian life.

Some authors wrote that women should stay and work at home and leave all the preaching, teaching, and leading to the men. In England during the 1800s, it was unheard of for women to speak during meetings, let alone preach. But from her readings, Catherine learned how God equipped and called many women to do those exact things. She knew God wasn't contradictory: the Creator wouldn't give women talents if he didn't intend those women to use them.

Catherine wrote a short, powerful book explaining her thoughts. Her reasoning was so compelling that her writing helped defend the careers of a few women speakers and helped shift the thinking about gender roles within the church.

But when it came to her own calling, Catherine was nervous and timid because being a female preacher was such a radical thing at that time. Instead, she poured all her talents and energy into cofounding the Salvation Army with her husband. The charitable organization provided food, shelter, and supplies to those who needed help. They also led numerous Bible classes and hosted gatherings that introduced God's love and salvation to those in need.

At the age of thirty-one, Catherine spoke publicly for the first time. During a church gathering, she shared her own experience finding the confidence to step into her calling. Her words were both challenging and encouraging to her listeners, and that talk launched an unprecedented speaking ministry. For the rest of her life, Catherine traveled around England as a popular preacher, using her compelling logic and engaging speeches to share God's truth and love with others. Her career helped fund the work of the Salvation Army, which by then had grown to serve the homeless and hungry in four countries.

We all have a God-given calling, a unique set of skills and passions that can make the world a better place. Catherine's story reminds us to trust ourselves and trust God's calling on our lives. As she said in her own words, "Whatever the particular call is, the particular sacrifice God asks you to make, the particular cross He wishes you to embrace; whatever the particular path He wants you to tread, will you rise up and say in your heart, 'Yes, Lord, I accept it; I submit; I yield?' [. . .] Oh but you say, 'I don't know what He will want next.' No, we none of us know that, but we know we shall be safe in His hands."[1]

Journaling Prompt

What kind of skills and passions do you have? What makes you nervous or timid about stepping into God's calling for you?

. . . .

. . . .

Beyond Brave

DAY THIRTY-EIGHT

Persistent Prayer

*Then Jesus told his disciples a
parable to show them that they should
always pray and not give up.*

LUKE 18:1

Have you ever wanted to ask God for something but thought it was too big or too crazy to happen? Or maybe you prayed about it for a few days and nothing happened, so you quit.

We've talked about how through Jesus, we can be brave and talk to God with confidence and honesty. But there's another level here we haven't explored yet: persistence. The most famous verse about persistence is 1 Thessalonians 5:17, which says, "Pray continually," meaning don't give up, don't stop bringing your requests to God.

But hundreds of years before that verse was penned, there was a woman who took this truth to heart.

Hannah was married a wealthy man named Elkanah. Their family followed God carefully, and every year they traveled to the temple at Shiloh to pray, worship, and offer gifts to God. But because Hannah didn't have any children, the other women in her community looked down on her, thinking God must not love her. Hannah longed to be able to hold and raise her own children. Year after year, when she and Elkanah went to the temple, she would ask God to give her a son. But year after year, nothing changed. She even promised God that if she had a baby boy, she would dedicate him to the temple so he could serve God alongside the priests. The emptiness in her arms brought her to tears, and she cried out to God time and time again. And then after a tearful day in the temple during her yearly trip, God answered her prayer. About nine months later she had a baby boy she named Samuel, which means "heard by God."

Hannah kept her promise, and so when Samuel was old enough, she took him to Shiloh, where he would live with the priests and study God's word. Samuel grew up to be a great prophet and a significant figure in Christian history, and served as a spiritual advisor to King David. And God continued to answer Hannah's persistent prayer. She had five more children.

Jesus told a story with the same idea. There was widow who was being mistreated by an adversary. She went to a judge and asked for his help. The judge refused, but she didn't take no for an answer. Every day, the widow went to the judge and made the same request: "Grant me justice against my adversary" (Luke 18:3). Finally, the judge became so annoyed that he gave her the help she needed. At the end of his story, Jesus said, "And will not God bring about justice for his chosen ones, who cry out to him day and night?" (verse 7).

God wants us to have the same boldness as the widow and the same persistence as Hannah. God doesn't want us to be nervous or shy, but to have the resilient faith to keep making our requests time after time until we see him move.

Journaling Prompt

Have you ever given up on bringing a request to God? How can you practice persistent prayer?

....

....

....

....

Beyond Brave

DAY THIRTY-NINE

Power of Compassion

*Yet the L*ORD *longs to be gracious
to you; therefore he will rise up
to show you compassion. For
the L*ORD *is a God of justice.*

ISAIAH 30:18

Though compassion may seem like a sweet and tender thing, story after story reminds us of its transforming power. Take Mary Kay Beard, for example.

By the age of twenty-seven, Mary Kay had created quite the criminal reputation for herself. After her first marriage ended in divorce, Mary Kay married a bank robber. Soon, she was helping run gambling cheats, then robbing banks herself. She even planned a prison break to free her husband. Even after her second husband abandoned her, she continued her criminal life. Eventually, she was on the FBI's most-wanted list and became a mafia target because she double-crossed them during a diamond heist. Her crimes caught up with her in 1972 when she was arrested and charged with eleven federal counts and thirty-five state counts of grand larceny and armed robbery and sentenced to twenty-one years in prison.

Serving time seemed like the lowest point in Mary Kay's life, but already God's compassion began to work in her heart. In prison, Mary Kay began to attend church services and even read the Bible. One evening in her cell, Mary Kay found Ezekiel 36:26: "I will give you a new heart and put a new spirit in you; I will remove from you your heart of stone and give you a heart of flesh." That verse caught her attention. Right then, Mary Kay prayed, "Okay, God, if you will do that for me . . . I will give the rest of my life back to you."[1]

Mary Kay used her time in prison to study the Bible and begin earning her master's degree. She also began to see the needs of those around her. What really caught her interest was how each Christmas, the female prisoners scraped together their meager possessions—toothbrushes and toothpaste, tiny shampoo bottles and bars of soap—and mailed them as gifts to their children back home.

After only six years, Mary Kay was released. She

finished her master's degree then joined a Christian ministry called Prison Fellowship. Part of her job was to organize a Christmas outreach program, and she knew exactly what would mean the most to those imprisoned moms. She created Angel Tree, a program that has served ten million children by providing Christmas gifts from their incarcerated parents. Today, Angel Tree continues to support the year-round emotional, physical, and spiritual needs of children who are so often forgotten by society. Not only did Mary Kay respond to God's compassion for her, she then carried that compassion on to touch the lives of millions. When it seems as though we've hit low points in our lives, let's ask for God's powerful compassion to soften our hearts and those around us.

Journaling Prompt

How have you seen the power of compassion at work in your life or the lives of those you know? Ask God to renew your heart so you can carry compassion on to others.

Beyond Brave

DAY FORTY

Apologize

*Love is patient, love is kind. It does not
envy, it does not boast, it is not proud.*

1 CORINTHIANS 13:4

Fewer things are as difficult as admitting you're wrong and apologizing. No matter how old you are, you could probably list a few instances when someone should have apologized for something they did or said, or didn't say or do, but they didn't. Situations like that breed bitterness for everyone.

We get into a habit of defending and justifying ourselves. We say things like, "Well, I didn't mean it that way," or "My heart was in the right place," or "My intention was to . . ." But all these phrases merely dodge the pain and embarrassment of saying, "I was wrong, I'm sorry."

It's painful and embarrassing because, deep down, we're all pretty prideful. We desperately want to be respected, and we want to impress others. Admitting we were wrong, that we hurt others, seems to do the opposite. But in reality, people who don't apologize actually lose the respect of others, while people who make true, heartfelt apologies actually earn more respect. Pretty ironic, right?

But more important than respect is the fact saying we're sorry gives us the chance to change our direction. "Turn from evil and do good; seek peace and pursue it," says Psalm 34:14. The practice of apologizing shows us what choices and habits in our lives are unhealthy or harmful, and it offers us the opportunity to make a conscious choice to do better.

And there's another side to apologizing that we don't always think about. When we admit our wrongs and try to do better, it's an act of love—the real kind of love that's sometimes hard but deeply beneficial. 1 Peter 4:8 says, "Above all, love each other deeply, because love covers over a multitude of sins." When we try to make up for the harm we've caused others, we put them above ourselves and our pride. It's one of the most selfless things we can do.

It's a courageous thing to admit we're wrong, to apologize without protecting or defending ourselves. It takes strength to humbly realize that we need to do better. But when we take this step—no matter how difficult it seems in the moment—we get to practice loving others and we grow a little more into the brave women we really are.

Journaling Prompt

Write about a time when you had to apologize. How did it feel and how did it help you grow as a person?

Beyond Brave

Christ in Everyone

*Live in harmony with one another.
Do not be proud, but be willing
to associate with people of low
position. Do not be conceited.*

ROMANS 12:16

Radical thinker and journalist Dorothy Day was born in New York in 1897 into a family of writers. Though her family was not religious, Dorothy loved the Psalms even at a young age. She began attending church when her family relocated to Chicago, even though her family and boyfriend didn't understand her beliefs.

In her twenties, Dorothy worked at newspapers staffed by atheists who thought religion had let people down. Dorothy felt pulled between their arguments and God's love. This tension was heightened when she observed wealthy Christians who paid for fancy cathedrals but didn't do much for the homeless and hungry. Thinking back on this time in her life, Dorothy wrote, "I felt keenly that God was more on the side of the hungry, the ragged, the unemployed, than on the side of the comfortable churchgoers who gave so little heed to the misery and the groaning of the poor. I prayed that some way would open up for me to do something . . ."[1]

Dorothy's prayer was answered when a fellow activist knocked on her door and described an idea for a radical, faith-based magazine that aimed to serve the hopeless and report on protests for social change and advocacy for the poor. In the first year, *The Catholic Worker* grew from 2,500 copies in the first printing to 100,000 copies every month. People without jobs or homes joined the newspaper and volunteered their time to help Dorothy with the work. And in response, Dorothy offered food and a place to stay in her own house. Dorothy's magazine garnered millions of readers who looked to her articles for inspiration and practical guidance in helping those around them.

When the Great Depression hit, *The Catholic Worker* became more than just a newspaper—the organization behind it also offered food to the hundreds of hungry, unemployed men every day. To the critics who thought she should focus on helping the "deserving poor" rather than the homeless, drunks, and addicts, Dorothy responded, "They live with us, they die with us [. . .] Once they are taken in, they become members of the family. Or rather they always were members of the family. They are our brothers and sisters in Christ."[2] By 1936, Dorothy's hospitality branched off into thirty-three additional Catholic Worker houses.

Whoever she was with, whether it was Mother Teresa (who she visited in India) or a homeless drunk, she sought to recognize God's image in that person and remember Christ's love for them. She saw common humanity in the rich and the poor. Even when she became famous, Dorothy never assumed she was more important than the homeless person sitting beside her. She firmly believed that her brothers and sisters in Christ included the enemy on the opposite side of the front line, the political parties and intellectual leaders she did not agree with, and the public who criticized her work.

Dorothy's life challenges us to reach across divisive lines and love those deemed unlovable. As she wrote, "I really only love God as much as I love the person I love the least."[3]

Beyond Brave

Journaling Prompt

What divisive lines do you see in the circles you live in?
How might you follow Dorothy's example of loving those
who we ignore, as well as those who think, believe, or live
differently?

DAY FORTY-TWO

Doubt

But when he, the Spirit of truth, comes,
he will guide you into all the truth.

JOHN 16:13

Doubt can be unnerving and uncomfortable. It can be scary to ask ourselves if we really believe what we say we believe, as it shakes our world and throws off our sense of normal.

We're afraid to voice our deep questions because we're worried about what we'll find when we look for answers.

But God is never afraid of doubt. Jesus never asked us to ignore our questions; he never turned a cold shoulder to anyone looking for the truth. For example, Jesus patiently answered the questions posed by the Samaritan woman at the well (John 4). When his followers didn't understand his teaching, he explained it to them (Luke 24:13–35). And when Thomas asked for evidence of Jesus' resurrection, Jesus appeared to him and showed him his scars (John 20:24–29).

Loving God with all of our selves includes our minds. To do that well, sometimes we have to ask serious questions. In the past, when believers thoughtfully challenged their religious views, their prayerful searching led the global church into a deeper understanding of God's love. It is through questions, discussions, studies, and prayer that we learn how to better align our hearts with God's. As Philippians 2:12–13 says, "Continue to work out your salvation with fear and trembling, for it is God who works in you to will and to act in order to fulfill his good purpose." God's good purpose is to draw us all into genuine, loving relationship. He does this even through our thoughts and doubts.

Jeremiah the prophet knew a real relationship with God didn't mean pushing aside his questions but instead openly talking about them with the One who knew everything. He prayed, "You are always righteous, LORD, when I bring a case before you. Yet I would speak with you about your justice" (Jeremiah 12:1), and then he went on to present a list of questions before God.

Like the woman at the well, and like Jeremiah, when

you have a doubt or a question about God and your faith, take them to God. Ask him to teach you and reveal to you the truth. Pray about it, keeping a humble heart. Remember that you're not alone in your search for understanding; God has given you a community of other believers, so talk about your questions with others so you will be able to help each other find answers. It takes courage to intentionally consider your doubts and patiently search for the truths. But when you do, your faith will be stronger. And God will be with you, patiently guiding and drawing you into a deeper understanding of truth and love.

Journaling Prompt

Write about your experience with doubt. As today's verse says, consider how the Holy Spirit might be working through your questions and thoughts to lead you toward a better understanding of God's love and truth.

Beyond Brave

DAY FORTY-THREE

God Is Our Help

Look to the LORD and his strength;
seek his face always.

1 CHRONICLES 16:11

Most of us are braver than we think we are. But even the most courageous people face moments when exhaustion or discouragement make it difficult to keep going. Susanna Wesley knew what this was like on a very personal level.

Susanna was born in 1669 as the youngest of twenty-five children. Susanna didn't have much formal schooling, but she did have a father who was an academic minister and access to lots of books and discussions, which gave her a well-rounded education. She then married Samuel, a minister like her father, and they had nine children.

Sadly, Samuel wasn't a successful minister. He didn't relate to his congregation and his controversial political views sparked strong dislike from the church community. Their home was burned twice, most likely by angry arsonists. Their son John almost died in one of the fires.

Sometimes Samuel would simply leave. Susanna had to raise and teach nine children and run the family farm all on her own for years. To make things worse, Samuel was terrible with money. Twice, he was imprisoned for his outstanding debts, and the constant financial strain put incredible stress on Susanna.

Exhaustion and discouragement were a consistent part of Susanna's reality, so she regularly sought God's peace and strength. There was hardly any privacy in her busy household, so each day she draped her large apron over her head to create a small, sacred space. In Scripture and in prayer, Susanna found God's comfort, wisdom, and help. Like we're told in Proverbs 18:10, Susanna discovered that "the name of the LORD is a fortified tower; the righteous run to it and are safe." Not only did her time in prayer console her own heart, God gave her profound wisdom and a strong teaching gift.

Susanna gave her children a quality education in both classical and biblical studies. She made sure her daughters learned the same subjects as her sons, a revolutionary idea at that time. She also created a rotating schedule so she could spend quality time with one of her children every night, another rare practice. And she shared the biblical truths God revealed to her with her children. Soon, about two hundred people from the community joined their family Bible study every week.

Two of her sons, John and Charles Wesley, carried on their mother's legacy by preaching the Bible to millions of listeners. Both became world-famous spiritual leaders whose teachings continue to influence our world today.

Susanna's legacy stands as a powerful reminder of both the personal and global impact of women who pray. When we feel tired and overwhelmed, when we don't know what to do, we can go back to the God who is always with us to find help and guidance.

Journaling Prompt

Think about situations in your life where you currently feel frustrated, exhausted, or discouraged. As you write about those experiences, ask God for the wisdom and help you need today.

Beyond Brave

DAY FORTY-FOUR

The Hope

The Father of compassion and the
God of all comfort, who comforts us
in all our troubles, so that we can
comfort those in any trouble.

2 CORINTHIANS 1:3–4

Most likely, you've already had to experience some pretty tough and painful things in your life. Sadly, you may be dealing with horrible brokenness right now.

Hopefully, the stories about the brave women in this book have showed you that you're not alone. They faced cultural limitations, obstacles due to the expectations of others, racism, prejudice, gender oppression, physical abuse and rape, emotional trauma, religious persecution, war, hunger, homelessness, sickness, and even death. The roads they walked were horribly painful, and yet they didn't give in to despair. They pushed against the obstacles, they grew beyond them, and they confronted them. The pain they experienced inspired them to do something that brought healing for themselves and others—and in the process they found freedom, rescued people in similar situations, gave voice to the voiceless, and battled bullies and oppressors.

To be clear, God doesn't cause evil things to happen or need them to occur in order to create good things. But God's redeeming power and transforming love can take any brokenness and turn it into something strong and beautiful. Yet even before that happens—even when we're still wondering how any good can come of our pain—God is with us. He says, "When you pass through the waters, I will be with you; and when you pass through the rivers, they will not sweep over you. When you walk through the fire, you will not be burned; the flames will not set you ablaze. For I am the LORD your God [. . .] You are precious and honored in my sight" (Isaiah 43:2–4).

Whatever pain you've experienced doesn't have to determine the rest of your life. You still have the power to decide what you will do next. There is so much life ahead of you, and you can still do amazing things with it—such as pursue dreams, create masterpieces, make a real difference in your community or even the world, and enjoy the brave and vibrant life you've been given. And here's the hope: that through the love and power of God who makes all things new, what feels weak and broken right now will become part of what makes you the resilient and powerful woman you were meant to be. Jeremiah 29:11 says it this way: "'For I know the plans I have for you,' declares the LORD, 'plans to prosper you and not to harm you, plans to give you hope and a future.'"

But here's a very important note: If you are a survivor of something particularly difficult, if you think you may be depressed, or if you feel like your emotional or mental health has been shaken, seek help from a counselor, a minister, a mom, or a woman you trust. Consider talking to someone trustworthy and safe about your experience. Not only should you never try to face those things alone, trusted and qualified people can help you find the peace and hope you need as you begin to move forward.

Journaling Prompt

Write a list of all the things you'd like to do in the future. Consider how your dreams and plans have been shaped or inspired by the difficulties you've lived through.

Beyond Brave

DAY FORTY-FIVE

Endurance for the Journey

May the God of hope fill you with all joy and peace as you trust in him, so that you may overflow with hope by the power of the Holy Spirit.

ROMANS 15:13

Teresa Sánchez de Cepeda y Ahumada didn't want to go to a convent. A rambunctious girl, Teresa was born in the 1500s into one of the wealthiest noble families of Spain. She was a local celebrity, frequenting parties and always dressing in the most opulent gowns. She loved music, dancing, and chatting with the social elite. Though she had a good sense of humor, Teresa could also be quite serious as a child. She often worried about the fate of her soul, and she was captivated by the stories of the saints and martyrs. As Teresa got older and became more focused on her appearance and social gatherings, her father and uncle became convinced her partying lifestyle would ruin her own reputation, so they sent her to a finishing school run by strict Augustinian nuns.

After completing her schooling, Teresa had the choice to marry or join a convent. At first, Teresa didn't think the convent life was a good fit for her. Though she respected the nuns, she never felt the same passion for devout prayer and worship as they did—try as she might. She feared that committing her whole life to a religious lifestyle would condemn her future to long hours of frustrated prayers, not to mention she would miss the joys of her old social life. But eventually, Teresa decided to join the Carmelite convent of Avila, which allowed for a far more relaxed and comfortable lifestyle than what the Augustinian nuns led. Still, Teresa's choice was more of duty and the fear of hell—she worried that if she didn't become a nun, she would never reach heaven.

Teresa still struggled with desires for her old life, and she missed wearing nice gowns and eating rich, flavorful foods. And no matter how much time she spent in prayer, she didn't experience any of the emotional connection to God the other nuns regularly experienced. But the habit of showing up each day to pray regardless of any reward—emotional or otherwise—strengthened her self-awareness and blunt honesty with God. And as years went by, Teresa no longer felt a desire for her old life and instead began to feel a profound love and passion for God. God gave her special insight into a fruitful prayer life, and Teresa shared these helpful reflections in *The Interior Castle,* a book that was passed among her fellow nuns to encourage their prayer life as well.

Ironically, Teresa's spiritual journey evolved so much that she became a key figure in the church reformation, which challenged the religious community of her day to give up worldly pleasures and instead seek a more devout faithfulness. She founded seventeen convents where the nuns walked barefoot as a sign they had left worldly pleasures behind in order to worship God completely.

For many, Saint Teresa is a relatable and comforting role model because she experienced the same tension between selfish desires and faithful commitment that we feel. Her life reminds us that following Christ is a journey over a lifetime, and if we show up each day, he will help us grow into a vibrant and deeply connected relationship with God.

Journaling Prompt

Reflect on your own unique spiritual journey. How have you already experienced growth in your relationship with God? What struggles do you still face in in your faith?

....
....
....
....
....
....
....
....
....
....
....
....
....
....
....
....
....
....
....
....
....

Expectant to See God

*See, I am doing a new thing! Now it
springs up; do you not perceive it?*

ISAIAH 43:19

I t's often difficult for us to see what God is doing in our lives, especially when we don't *expect* to see anything. We often pray, quickly running down a list of requests, then open our eyes and forget to watch for God's response. But God does move in our worlds, more than we realize. Anna saw this in a very literal way.

Luke 2 tells us the story of Anna, a prophet at the turn of the first century. She had lived a long, sometimes hard life. She lost her husband after only seven years of marriage. She had no children, which in cultural terms isolated her from the other women. Anna also lived during the reign of Herod the Great, a volatile and murderous ruler. On top of those details, there was corruption and power struggles between the religious leaders of Anna's day.

Even though Anna's life hadn't turned out the way she had hoped, she knew God was still moving, bringing restoration and healing to her people, and she longed to see it. She *expected* to see it.

Anna spent all her time in the temple and rarely left; and if she was allowed to live at the temple, it was a very honorable thing because the apartments there were usually set aside for men. People took notice of the intimate relationship she had with God and respected her strong faith. For decades she spent all her days and nights in prayer and worship. Her resilient faithfulness reminds us of Psalm 130:5–6: "I wait for the Lord, my whole being waits, and in his word I put my hope. I wait for the Lord more than watchmen wait for the morning."

One day, a young couple came into the temple carrying a baby boy. From all her years longing and expecting to see God, she was able to recognize the baby boy as Jesus Christ, the Son of God. Luke 2:38 tells us that, "Coming up to them at that very moment, she gave thanks to God and spoke about the child to all who were looking forward to the redemption of Jerusalem." For the rest of her life, she

Expectant to See God

boldly shared the news that the hope of humanity, the very presence of God, had come at last.

Because she spent so much time listening and watching for God's presence, Anna was one of the first people to recognize Jesus as he really was. As God says in Jeremiah 29:13–14, "You will seek me and find me when you seek me with all your heart. I will be found by you."

Like Anna, let's be expectant, watching to see how God is moving in our lives and in our worlds.

Journaling Prompt

Write about a time when you feel you saw God at work in your life. How might you better remember to watch for God at work in the future?

(blank journaling lines)

Beyond Brave

DAY FORTY-SEVEN

A God So Big

Can you fathom the mysteries of God?
Can you probe the limits of the Almighty?
They are higher than the heavens above.

JOB 11:7–8

As a collective group, humans are uncomfortable with mess, contradictions, the unknown, and paradox. Life presents us with so many dichotomies—life and death, art and science, true and false. And try as we might to categorize and make sense of it all, life remains a messy complexity. Which is why Madeleine L'Engle is such an encouraging figure to us today.

Like most of us, Madeleine faced many paradoxes in her lifetime—the care and yet neglect of parents who kept extremely busy with their social lives, a love for learning but a stressful and lonely experience at school, a long marriage that was both devoted and also less than her ideal at times, and the joys of children and grandchildren and the grief and sorrow when their lives were threatened by illness and injury.

Madeleine had a deep appreciation for the stories of the Bible, the prayers of the saints, and the church creeds. Especially in her later life, she did morning and evening devotions. She was drawn to the vast, unlimitable power of the Divine, and she valued how art, Scripture, and science all revealed unique aspects of the mystery of God. Unlike many of her fellow Christians and readers who were uncomfortable with messy mysteries and paradoxes, Madeleine found inspiration and comfort in a God who is big enough to hold the whole world, and is able to love and redeem it despite all its darkness amidst the light. She knew that as we navigate this life and learn to hold opposites together, we will discover how vibrant and dynamic God really is.

A writer even as a child, Madeleine wrote prolifically. Yet her breakout novel, *A Wrinkle in Time*, was rejected over two dozen times because, just like herself, her writing didn't fit nicely into the preexisting categories. Her story was written for children but dealt with serious matters of evil and loss. She melded fiction with fantasy. And her main character is not the typical heroine; Meg Murry is nerdy and awkward, and saves not only herself but the whole planet.

After years of trying to get *A Wrinkle in Time* published, Madeleine tried to quit writing several times, but she couldn't. She decided that she would keep writing anyway, for the love of the craft, even if she was never published again. Four years after that decision, *A Wrinkle in Time* was finally published and won awards. Madeleine went on to write more than sixty books of fiction, science fiction, nonfiction, poetry, and essays.

In each of her books, Madeleine gracefully reminds us not to fear the paradoxes of this messy life. She helps us cultivate a courageous faith in a God so big and so wonderful that there is ample room for both questions and truths, anger and joy, death and life, brokenness and beauty.

Journaling Prompt

In what ways have you seen the fear of the unknown limit your own life or the lives of others? How might the paradoxes and messiness of life inspire you to see God in a more expansive way?

Beyond Brave

DAY FORTY-EIGHT

For the Glory of God

*Never be lacking in zeal, but keep
your spiritual fervor, serving the Lord.
[...] Share with the Lord's people who
are in need. Practice hospitality.*

ROMANS 12:11, 13

Lydia was a highly respected businesswoman during the first century. She was a successful entrepreneur who was also smart, independent, confident, generous, welcoming to others, and tenderhearted.

Acts 16:11–15, 40 tells us about Lydia's life in Philippi, an important and affluent Roman city near the coast of the Aegean Sea. Lydia was a dealer in purple cloth, a luxury item in those days that was aimed at the upper class. The type of purple-reddish color she sold was famous because it didn't fade as easily as other cloth colors and became brighter with sunlight. Senior government officials and royalty would edge their white clothes with a strip of Lydia's cloth, but only the emperors could wear a garment of solid purple. As a seller of such a valuable product, Lydia became wealthy.

Even though Lydia's culture worshiped many gods, she worshiped the one true God. The Bible tells us she became such a passionate believer that she shared her faith with her family, household servants, and business staff. She often gathered with other women by the riverside to pray and worship together.

But no one had told Lydia about Jesus Christ and the salvation he brought. So one day, as she gathered with other women near a river, Paul and Silas began sharing the teachings and story of Jesus. Acts 16:14 says, "The Lord opened her heart to respond to Paul's message." She asked Paul to baptize her and all the believers in her household. Then she opened her home to Paul and Silas to use as a base for their ministry, and it became a central meeting place for the church in Philippi.

With Lydia's natural talents for leadership, organization, and strategic thinking, she played a major role in building up the first Christian community in modern-day Europe. God blessed her work, and with the connections

For the Glory of God

and finances she received from her successful business, she helped others. After Paul and Silas left to continue preaching the gospel to other nations, it was Lydia's church that provided for their travel and living expenses. Paul wrote, "As you Philippians know, in the early days of your acquaintance with the gospel, when I set out from Macedonia, not one church shared with me in the matter of giving and receiving, except you only; [. . .] I am amply supplied, now that I have received from Epaphroditus the gifts you sent. They are a fragrant offering, an acceptable sacrifice, pleasing to God" (Philippians 4:15, 18).

Today, Lydia is considered "Equal to the apostles" by Orthodox churches. She continues to be an example of a woman who used everything she had—her career, her business smarts, her leadership strength, and her wealth— for the glory of God.

Journaling Prompt

How does Lydia's example change the way you think about vocation and work?

....

....

....

Beyond Brave

God-Given Desires

*And we know that in all things God works
for the good of those who love him, who
have been called according to his purpose.*

ROMANS 8:28

As passionate women, we care a lot about living out
our life purpose. We long to do something useful
and to make a difference. This desire is a significant and
worthy goal, yet it's often difficult to know how to go
about achieving it.

At fifteen years old, Amy Carmichael became a
Christian and grew a passion to share God's love with
others. In her home city of Belfast, Ireland, she started a
Sunday Bible class for the girls who worked long hours in
the city mills. Over almost ten years, Amy's little ministry

expanded to five hundred girls each week, and grew so much that they needed a new building.

Amy felt a desire to do more and sensed God calling her to the missions field. She applied for a position and eventually traveled to India to begin a different kind of work.

There, Amy met a young girl who had been forced into temple prostitution, a religious practice in that culture. Amy provided shelter for the young girl and protected her from those who wanted to return her to the temple. This launched Amy's new ministry—a sanctuary for rescued girls. Throughout the fifty-five years she worked in India, mostly without any kind of financial help, Amy saved and provided for hundreds of young women. She often traveled miles and miles to save just one girl from suffering. They called her *Amma*, which means "mother."

In her sixties, a terrible fall left Amy bedridden with serious injuries. She could no longer do the same work, but by then she had a team of missionaries to run the sanctuary. She turned to her other passion: writing. She published seventeen books and many other literary works about God's work in India, missions, helping others even when it's difficult, and living out the teachings of Jesus. This third ministry inspired readers around the world to go out and share God's love with those who had never

heard about it before. It's impossible to know just how many lives were changed throughout Amy's life.

As Amy's example shows us, our God-given desires look different at various points in our lives—she was a Bible teacher and mentor, a liberator and protector, and then an inspiring storyteller. Yet every step was important. In each role, God partnered with Amy to make the world a better place. She wrote, "It is a safe thing to trust Him to fulfill the desire which He creates."[1] We don't have to know what our purpose looks like for the rest of our lives. We simply follow what we know to do next and pay attention to the desires God has given us.

Journaling Prompt

What brave desires has God given you? What a first step can you take this year?

. . . .

. . . .

. . . .

. . . .

. . . .

. . . .

. . . .

Beyond Brave

DAY FIFTY

Called to the Extraordinary

Grant me a willing spirit, to sustain me.

PSALM 51:12

If someone had told seven-year-old Wilma Rudolph she would eventually leave her leg brace behind and become the world's fastest woman, I don't think she would have believed them. If you had told a younger Rosa Parks that one day she would kickstart a national campaign and be called "mother of the freedom movement," she probably would have thought you were crazy.

God is always picking unexpected people to do unexpected things. All throughout time—from the stories of the Bible to today—God calls on normal people to do

207

extraordinary things. This is both challenging and relieving to us.

It's challenging because no one is off the hook. Each one of us is charged to do what God has called us to do, even if we think what God has called us to do is crazy or impossible.

And it's relieving because we don't have to feel qualified. Catherine Booth was shy about her own calling to be a speaker, and Catherine of Siena struggled with anorexia her whole life. For years, Teresa of Avila showed up to pray without feeling an emotional connection with God, and Mother Teresa fought against doubt and loneliness even while the world recognized her as a saint. Who would feel qualified to raise the Son of God, as Mary was called to do? But we don't have to feel qualified.

Madeleine L'Engle, who received over twenty-four rejections and numerous critiques from publishers before her breakout novel became a bestseller, later wrote, "Slowly I have realized that I do not have to be qualified to do what I am asked to do, that I just have to go ahead and do it, even if I can't do it as well as I think it ought to be done. This is one of the most liberating lessons of my life."[1]

Our culture cares a lot about credentials, about people being certified and approved to do whatever job they set out to accomplish. But the qualifications the world looks

Called to the Extraordinary

for don't matter as much to God. 1 Corinthians 1:25 says, "For the foolishness of God is wiser than human wisdom, and the weakness of God is stronger than human strength."

What God counts as qualifications are a love for Jesus Christ and faith in his presence. God looks for a willing spirit that—though it feels scared, weak, or inadequate—tries to do its best nonetheless. Because as 2 Corinthians 12:9 reminds us, God's wonderful grace and extraordinary power shines through our weakness to achieve unexpected things.

Journaling Prompt

How does today's devotion change the way you think about your own qualifications? Consider how you've seen God do unexpected things in your life already.

Beyond Brave

DAY FIFTY-ONE

Keep Your Focus

*And what does the L*ORD* require of*
you? To act justly and to love mercy
and to walk humbly with your God.

MICAH 6:8

Living as a Christian today is often complicated. Political issues, cultural debates, and personal tensions keep us searching for how to live out our faith in truth and love. Too often, we lose sight of the important yet simple basics of our faith. One of the best examples of faithfully keeping the basics in mind is the prolific poet and songwriter Fanny Crosby.

In 1820, when Fanny was just six weeks old, her parents realized she was blind. Even as a child, though, Fanny was very positive and considered her blindness a gift from

God. Growing up, her mother and grandmother helped Fanny memorize large sections of the Bible, and through this she developed a love for poetry. Starting at age eight, Fanny wrote her own poems, and in her twenties, major publications started featuring her work.

Fanny used her writing as a call for political, social, and educational reform. It was clear she had a heart for those living in poverty and others who couldn't speak up for themselves. But it wasn't until her thirties that Fanny truly grasped the power of God's love for her. Her renewed faith led her to become one of the most prolific religious song writers of all time.

Highly educated, Fanny had the skill and training to compose complex melodies and intricate lyrics, but she felt called to share the message of God's love very simply so that people of all education levels could understand it. She set a personal goal of bringing a million people to Christ through her work, and before sitting down to write each hymn, she first prayed for God's inspiration. By the end of her career, she had written about eight thousand songs, including "Blessed Assurance," "To God be the Glory," and "Draw Me Nearer."

Fanny and her husband had enough money to live in a nice home in New York, but instead they lived in a cramped apartment in a poorer district. They gave all they could to those in need, and Fanny often met with people struggling with addictions in order to give them encouragement and remind them they were loved. She said, "You can't save a man by telling him of his sins. He knows them already. Tell him there is pardon and love waiting for him. Win his confidence and make him understand that you believe in him, and never give him up."[1]

There were many complicated issues in Fanny's day, yet she always kept her focus on the important practices of helping others and sharing God's love. She is a beautiful picture of what it looks like to follow Jesus in living out Isaiah 61:1: "The Spirit of the Sovereign LORD is on me, because the LORD has anointed me to proclaim good news to the poor."

Journaling Prompt

Reflect on Fanny's legacy. What stood out to you about Fanny's simple yet powerful faith? How can you keep your focus on what's really important?

Beyond Brave

God's Timing

*He has made everything beautiful in
its time. He has also set eternity in the
human heart; yet no one can fathom what
God has done from beginning to end.*

ECCLESIASTES 3:11

Do you ever get the feeling your life is already planned out for you? American culture can often feel like a schedule that is forced upon us. As if it's a template that everyone follows, we all aim to study hard, get good grades, get the degree, land that awesome job, climb the corporate ladder, meet Mister Awesome, get married, have kids, and then travel and retire happily. It's a fine plan, except when it doesn't work.

Maybe school isn't everything you thought it would

be, or deciding on the right job path is taking longer for you than it did for your friends; maybe an injury or illness delayed your goals, or Mister Awesome turned out to be Mister Not. When we miss a step, it can feel as though we've lost our footing and fallen behind. We may fear we've ruined our life's purpose. But that's a lie. Because the template is only that—a template. It's a manmade, popular guide, but it was never designed to be the best plan for *you*.

God has given you a unique calling, a special purpose. And there's nothing that can ruin God's beautiful plan for you. As Job 42:2 says, "I know that you (God) can do all things; no purpose of yours can be thwarted." Nothing can spoil or take away your God-given purpose—not even you. A missed opportunity, a failed job, a plan that didn't work, or a bad decision will not interrupt God's distinct plan for your life.

Your life won't look like everyone else's because it's not supposed to. Some of us don't want to get married, some of us were never made to work in a cubicle, some of us have struck out on a path all our own. You may not follow the same timeline as your friends or family members, and that's okay. Just like trees, we all grow differently, produce different fruits, and are all beautiful in unique ways.

Philippians 1:6 reminds us that "he (God) who began

a good work in you will carry it on to completion until the day of Christ Jesus." God is patient and faithful. Even now, you're growing in the way you were made to, within the timeframe God has in mind. It's okay to be frustrated or discontent, because that too is a sign you're growing. So take a breath, trust your own process, and trust God's perfect timing for you.

Journaling Prompt

Write about a time when your plans seemed ruined. What did that experience teach you or how did it help you grow?

Beyond Brave

DAY FIFTY-THREE

Sing to the Lᴏʀᴅ, all the earth; proclaim
his salvation day after day.

1 CHRONICLES 16:23

In our fast-paced, productivity-craving world, it can be easy to remain so focused on working hard and being strong that we lose sight of the power of celebration.

Miriam was one of the spunkiest women in the Bible. We have several stories about her in Exodus. She was the sister of Moses during a time when the Hebrews were slaves in Egypt. To limit the number of Hebrews living and working in Egypt, the pharaoh ordered the deaths of all their baby boys. Miriam's mom placed Moses in a waterproof basket and pushed him gently into the river, hoping someone would find him and care for him. But young Miriam followed the basket, and when the pharaoh's daughter picked her little brother up, Miriam struck a deal with her so that her mom could care for Moses.

Years later, as an adult, God sent Moses to bring freedom to all the Hebrews. And when everyone else worried whether they could trust Moses, Miriam was one of the first people to welcome him. Then Miriam worked as one of Moses' advisors and helped alongside him as they left Egypt, formed their own nation, followed God through the desert, and then settled into the coastland along the Mediterranean Sea.

But even though Miriam had loads of responsibility and a ton of work on her plate, she didn't forget to celebrate the good things. When God led the Hebrews through the Red Sea to freedom, Miriam kicked off a spontaneous party. "Then Miriam the prophet, Aaron's sister, took a timbrel in her hand, and all the women followed her, with timbrels and dancing. Miriam sang to them: 'Sing to the LORD, for he is highly exalted'" (Exodus 15:20–21).

People are often surprised to learn just how many celebrations are found in the Bible and celebrated in the Christian calendar. To name just a few, Christmas celebrates the birth of Christ; Palm Sunday, Good Friday, and Easter celebrate Jesus' death and resurrection and the relationship we now enjoy with God; Purim and Passover are Jewish holidays celebrating God's rescuing power; Pentecost is a holiday when we celebrate God sending his Holy Spirit to lead and guide believers of Christ. In fact, the Bible ends with a feast, where God and all believers throughout time and from around the world are finally joined together to celebrate. Clearly, celebrations are important to God.

Like Miriam showed through her son, enjoying the good things helps us recognize how God is working in our lives. Holidays help us remember year to year how faithful and powerful God is. And when we celebrate, we become a source of joyful strength, encouraging and helping others see the good God has done in their lives too.

Journaling Prompt

How do you generally enjoy the good things—big or small—in your life? How can you practice celebrating God's gifts in your daily life more often?

....

....

....

....

....

Beyond Brave

DAY FIFTY-FOUR

Keep Trying

*The LORD makes firm the steps of the
one who delights in him; though he
may stumble, he will not fall, for the
LORD upholds him with his hand.*

PSALM 37:23–24

The minute we begin to practice living bravely, we find resistance. Maybe you've already experienced this. You speak up only to get talked over, you stand your ground only to be pushed around, you overcome an obstacle only to find three more. And if we're shooting for perfection, this kind of constant resistance is paralyzing. So it's a good thing bravery is not about perfection. It's about growth.

This is a hard message for most of us to hear today,

especially in light of our achievement-crazy, success-oriented, and perfectionistic society. This intense perspective causes most of us to believe that unless we become good at something quickly, it's not worth trying. If you can't make the team, don't play. If your photography skills were critiqued, find a new hobby. If you love running but you're not fast, don't even bother. In reality, though, this perspective is rather ridiculous.

When a toddler is first learning how to draw, we don't criticize them for not creating a masterpiece fit for a museum. We don't mock their skill level. No, we all clap and celebrate their creativity. We hang the colorful doodles on the fridge because we want to honor their work and progress. What if we treated ourselves the same way? Instead of getting frustrated at ourselves for not being perfectly brave enough, not feeling confident 100 percent of the time, or not pushing ourselves past the limit at every chance, what if we learned to celebrate our baby steps?

Every time we try something, we grow a little—especially if we fail. Failure reveals our weak points, teaches us what to do better next time, and builds our endurance. Failure is an essential part of growing toward success. Jeremiah 8:4 reminds us, "When people fall down, do they not get up? When someone turns away, do they not return?" and Galatians 6:9 says, "Let us not become weary in doing good, for at the proper time we will reap a harvest if we do not give up." Don't grow weary of trying, because trying and failing is better than not trying. Doing something halfway is better than not doing it any way. Doing something poorly is better than not doing it at all.

As you strengthen your courage and practice being brave, you will experience failure. There will be times when you could have done something better. But that's a good sign, because only someone who is becoming braver would notice that they have room to grow. So take baby steps, do things halfway until you can do them all the way. Be brave enough to keep trying.

Journaling Prompt

Reflect on a time when you experienced resistance or failure in some way. What small, baby-sized step could you make today toward trying again?

....

....

....

....

....

....

Beyond Brave

DAY FIFTY-FIVE

Mentor Others

*And let us consider how we may spur one
another on toward love and good deeds.*

HEBREWS 10:24

B ravery is contagious. As we've seen in these stories,
when women step in and own their courage, others
see it and want to do the same. Maybe you haven't noticed
yet, but people look up to you too.

Naomi didn't realize at first how much her daughter-
in-law Ruth looked up to her. We find their story in the
book of Ruth. There wasn't enough food in Bethlehem
because of a famine, so Naomi, her husband, and her two
sons had moved to Moab to try to make a living there.
Naomi's sons fell in love and got married, and things were

looking up. But then tragedy struck: Naomi's husband and both of her sons died.

With few other options, Naomi decided to go back to her friends and family in Bethlehem. She told her daughters-in-law, "Go back, each of you, to your mother's home. May the LORD show you kindness, as you have shown kindness to your dead husbands and to me" (Ruth 1:8).

But Ruth loved and admired Naomi. "Where you go I will go, and where you stay I will stay. Your people will be my people and your God my God" (Ruth 1:16).

So Naomi and Ruth journeyed together to Bethlehem. As they started a new life together, Naomi mentored and encouraged Ruth as Ruth found a job, developed a relationship with God, and adapted to her new culture. Eventually, Ruth met a man named Boaz, and Naomi gave her helpful advice for starting that new relationship. Because of that advice, Ruth and Boaz married and had a son. The book of Ruth closes with a sweet picture of Naomi, her lonely and broken heart happy again as she holds her new grandson.

We all have people like Ruth in our lives who need our encouragement. We all have people in our lives who look up to us. Maybe for you, it's a younger or older sibling, your friends, teammates, a coworker, or someone whose admiration you haven't noticed yet. Sometimes we push others away when they try to follow us, like Naomi did at first. But God calls us to build them up, encourage them, and help them. 1 Timothy 4:12 says that no matter how old you are, you should set an example for others in the way you talk and behave, and through your relationship with God.

We don't have to be perfect to help others learn to be brave. In fact, it's often during the times we're struggling, like when Naomi lost her husband, that others around us learn the most.

As Naomi discovered, it's a beautiful thing to be able to mentor others. It's a special gift when you let others join you to see how you're learning and growing, and in turn help them learn and grow too.

Journaling Prompt

Who looks up to you? How can you encourage them or share with them something you've learned?

Beyond Brave

DAY FIFTY-SIX

Leadership

*Now Deborah, a prophet, the wife of
Lappidoth, was leading Israel at that time.
She held court under the Palm of Deborah.*

JUDGES 4:4–5

The older we get, the more opportunities we have to be leaders in our schools, families, communities, workplaces, and churches. There are all sorts of new ideas and theories on how to lead well, but the oldest and truest principle for leading well is prayer.

Early on in Israel's history, before there were any kings, judges served as guides. Individuals mediated peace, led military campaigns, and sought God's wisdom whenever crises or disputes came up. Israel's fourth judge was a strong woman named Deborah.

It was extremely rare for women to be military and political leaders like Deborah. In fact, of all the judges that are named in the Bible, Deborah is the only woman. It was also rare for women to be prophets—respected individuals who voiced God's will to others. But Deborah was both.

Deborah was respected for her great wisdom. As a prophet, she constantly prayed and carefully listened to God's voice, then shared God's instructions, encouraging reminders, and hard truths with her people. When anyone had an argument or couldn't come to an agreement, they hiked into the hill country, where Deborah sat under a date palm tree. There, she would help them find a peaceful solution.

When a powerful neighboring kingdom oppressed Israel, Deborah prayed, and God gave her a plan for defending their land and pushing back the enemy. As part of that plan, Deborah called an army together. She wasn't a soldier, but the general had such faith in her relationship with God that he insisted she ride alongside him. He and the people knew that if Deborah was with them, God was with them. Judges 4 tells about that epic battle and how God helped a group of farmers and shepherds defeat an army with nine hundred iron chariots.

The type of strong and wise leadership Deborah possessed flowed naturally from her relationship with God.

As she spent time in God's presence and sought God's wisdom, she became equipped with the knowledge to guide and serve others. Her prayer life gave her such confidence in God that her physical presence strengthened the faith of her people.

Whether you serve as a leader in an official role or you work behind the scenes, you have more capacity than you realize to encourage and guide others. And the more you seek God's presence, the more you will be able to lead others in strength and wisdom.

Journaling Prompt

In what circles do you find yourself serving as a leader in some capacity/where do you have influence? Take some time today to write down those opportunities, and ask God for help in giving others wisdom and guidance.

Beyond Brave

DAY FIFTY-SEVEN

Lifelong Learners

*The Holy Spirit, whom the Father
will send in my name, will teach
you all things and will remind you
of everything I have said to you.*

JOHN 14:26

In the first few stages of our lives, we're focused on learning all we can so we eventually have all the answers. We take this approach with school, relationships, work, and faith. The thought is, "One day, I'll have it all figured out." But that day never comes. Instead, the braver choice is a decision to be lifelong learners, women who keep their minds open and dedicate themselves to a lifetime of growth—like Kathleen Lonsdale.

A gifted academic, Kathleen excelled in school. And

though she lived in the 1900s, there were still not as many opportunities for women as there were for men. In order to follow her interests in physics, chemistry, and mathematics, Kathleen had to transfer from her all-girl's high school just outside London, England, to the boy's high school. She quickly grew comfortable with being a pioneer among her peers and continued to achieve excellent grades. She went on to graduate from the University of London with the highest marks in physics in ten years.

After college, Kathleen was recruited to join a research team studying the structure of molecules. She married a few years later and developed scientific formulas from home while she raised her three children; but once they reached school age she let her desire to continue learning lead her back into full-time research.

Kathleen was raised a Baptist during the completion of the first World War. When the second World War started in her thirties, Kathleen felt a moral resistance to the death and violence that encompasses war. She and her husband converted to Quakerism, which promotes an anti-war, nonviolent stance. Because of her pacifist beliefs, Kathleen refused to register for civil defense duties and protested the fine. As a result, she served a month in a women's prison, where she experienced the poor conditions firsthand. Once released, Kathleen argued for better, cleaner, and more humane treatment of prisoners.

A woman of intellect and wit, Kathleen made great contributions to both science and social reform. She played an essential role in developing the field of crystallography and the use of X-ray in chemistry and physics. She was respected for her groundbreaking research papers. She was the first female to lead many of the associations she served. As an energetic follower of Jesus, she opened her home to World War II refugees, campaigned against the use of nuclear bombs and the death toll that would inevitably result, and wrote and spoke on strategies to end war and promote peace. In war-torn Europe at that time, her straightforward voice was revolutionary.

Kathleen knew that in science and faith, you never arrive at a perfect, solidified understanding; instead, we're always learning and growing. She tried to maintain a curious mind that was ready to learn and adapt to new insights. She said, "I believe if we knew all the answers there would be no point in carrying out scientific research. Because we do not, it is stimulating, exciting, challenging. So too is the Christian life, lived experimentally. If we knew all the answers it would not be nearly such fun."[1]

Journaling Prompt

In what way would you like to grow in your spiritual life? How might you be able to cultivate a curious heart and practice a willingness to grow alongside the insights you discover about others and God?

. . . .

. . . .

. . . .

. . . .

. . . .

. . . .

. . . .

. . . .

. . . .

. . . .

. . . .

. . . .

. . . .

. . . .

. . . .

. . . .

. . . .

. . . .

. . . .

DAY FIFTY-EIGHT

A Rich Legacy

*For though the righteous fall seven
times, they rise again, but the wicked
stumble when calamity strikes.*

PROVERBS 24:16

Already we've studied the amazing legacies of many brave women. But we don't have to look too far to find inspiring women in our own lives.

Most likely, the women in your life have overcome many difficulties—depression, hopelessness, financial obstacles, health issues, mental health struggles, career challenges, and learning disabilities. The women around you have overcome tragedy, abuse, injustice, and mistreatment. They've stood their ground, spoken the truth when it wasn't popular, challenged false beliefs, overturned

Beyond Brave

oppressive systems, fought for the weak, and defended those who were overlooked. Look at your mom, grandmother, great-grandmother, godmother, aunt, cousins, friends, your friends' moms, teachers, and mentors, and you'll see women who have used their skills, knowledge, passions, time, and generosity to make the world a better place.

As you consider the women in your community, you can probably list their mistakes too. Maybe you've witnessed times when fear or the need for control led them to make unhealthy choices. And if you're being honest, you could recall the times when the women in your life hurt you in serious ways. Forgotten promises, harsh words, and important moments when the women we look up to weren't there for us only affirm what *not* to do. None of us are perfect. We all see the blemishes in ourselves and others.

Each of the heroines in this book had flaws as well—they had their issues in addition to their triumphs. Since they were humans just like us, they probably hurt someone at some point. But bravery doesn't ignore the truth of our weaknesses. It doesn't ignore the weaknesses of others, refusing to see nothing but the positive. That's simply unrealistic. The harder, more courageous way forward is to acknowledge the good and the not so good in each one of us.

A Rich Legacy

As we grow, we gain the maturity to see the complicated stories of the women around us as rounded examples for our own lives: we can be inspired by their bravery and learn from their mistakes. Like Hebrews 13:7 says, "Remember your leaders, who spoke the word of God to you. Consider the outcome of their way of life and imitate their faith." Each woman in our lives is a lesson to us about what to do, what not to do, and what to strive for. They present the truth about real courage, which at times looks a lot like facing a challenge while scared and losing, but staying in the fight anyway.

So as you look to grow into the capable woman you were made to be, look carefully at the women closest to you—learn from their mistakes and celebrate their strength. Their stories give you a rich legacy that will guide you into true bravery.

Journaling Prompt

Write about the women closest to you. How have their lives taught you about bravery?

....

....

....

Beyond Brave

Ezer

The LORD God said, "It is not good
for the man to be alone. I will make
a helper (Ezer) suitable for him."

GENESIS 2:18

There is a stunningly powerful Hebrew word used to describe women in Genesis: *Ezer-Kenegdo.* God uses it to describe Eve when he first creates the female gender. Many Bible scholars translate this word into English as *helper, helpmate,* or *suitable companion.* These are fine words in many respects—helping is a wonderful act and essential to humanity—but these words don't capture the full weight and power behind *Ezer.*

As close to the original meaning that we can get in English, *Ezer-Kenegdo* means "strong and perfect warrior-helper." *Ezer* is mentioned more than twenty-one times in the Bible; twice for women (Genesis 2:18 and 20), three times for the nations that rescued Israel when Israel was under attack, and sixteen times for our warrior God who rescues. This word is powerful, almost always used in the context of battle or wars or military rescue. Here's just a taste of what *Ezer* means:

> Quick to deliver (Psalm 70:5)
> Strong warrior (Psalm 89:19)
> Trustworthy defender (Psalm 115:9)
> Inspires hope (Psalm 146:5)
> A guard and sentry (Psalm 33:18)
> A shield and glorious sword (Deuteronomy 33:29)

This is epic, brave language about our warrior God. *Ezer* is one way to describe the redemptive work God has been doing in the world since sin entered the scene. All throughout the Bible, God is constantly rescuing, protecting, and, yes, helping humankind. And it's Jesus, our warrior God in human form, who rescues all of humanity from the death of sin and delivers us into God's love and presence.

And this is the identity that God gave to us women. This is who we are created to be.

It's a powerful calling that applies to every stage of our lives. Like Jesus, we get to partner with God in redemptive work here on earth. We can be strong girls who train our bodies and minds, who stand up to bullies and help those in need. We can be young warriors who forge new businesses that work to make the world a better place. We can be scientists who discover new ways to protect humanity from disease and disaster. We can rescue those in physical, emotional, or spiritual danger. We can be trustworthy guards and teachers who train others to fulfill their own callings. And even when our hair has turned white with age, we can still fight to bring hope and peace to others.

As women of God, we are so much more than mere assistants and helpers. We weren't created simply as companions. From the very beginning, we were created to be God's warriors, powerful rescuers for all creation.

Journaling Prompt

How does *Ezer* change the way you think about your identity now and your future self? What does it mean to you that God has given you this powerful calling?

. . . .

. . . .

Beyond Brave

DAY SIXTY

Don't Wait

*May the God of hope fill you with all
joy and peace as you trust in him,
so that you may overflow with hope
by the power of the Holy Spirit.*

ROMANS 15:13

You can watch scary movies at thirteen, get your driver's license at sixteen, vote at eighteen, drink alcohol at twenty-one, rent a car at twenty-five . . . these are the legal milestones along the way as you grow into adulthood. And as with each of these age markers, we tend to wait until we're older before we start thinking about the contribution we want to make on the world. But there's no real reason for this idea. In fact, there are a lot of really good reasons why you shouldn't wait at all.

Ruby Bridges was only six when her brave courage inspired a nation struggling with racism.

Fanny Crosby was eight when she started writing poetry, and a teenager when her work began to be published.

At fifteen, Amy Carmichael started her Sunday Bible class.

Mary was in her early teens when she became the mother of Jesus.

Mother Teresa was eighteen years old when she entered the convent and began her charitable work.

And twenty-year-old Sophie Scholl protested the Nazi regime and died defending the lives of others.

Now more than ever, young women are taking a stand, speaking out, and banding together to start their own organizations, protest, attend rallies, publish their ideas, and raise funds to make big differences around the world.

No matter what your age is, you don't need special permission to get started, to set an example, make a change, or get involved. You are already a contender. You are already an active and valued member of the human race. The world needs your passions, your ideas, your perspectives, your voice, and your contributions.

This is true even if others tell you that you're too young to do anything serious, or tease you for your age, or refuse to listen to you. When you take yourself seriously, others will catch on and take you seriously too. As Paul wrote to his young student, "Don't let anyone look down on you because you are young, but set an example for the believers in speech, in conduct, in love, in faith and in purity" (1 Timothy 4:12).

God loves and empowers believers of every age. In fact, your young age might just be what challenges and inspires others. When people see young women living out their confident calling, speaking truth, standing up for others, and striving to make the world a brighter place, they can't help but be inspired and hopefully start living their own brave lives.

Journaling Prompt

How might you set an example to others in speech, behavior, love, faith, and purity as 1 Timothy 4:12 says? As you write, ask God for wisdom and courage to start living today as strong woman of God.

Beyond Brave

Endnotes

Day Seven: Using Our Gifts
1. *Harriet Beecher Stowe: A Life*, Joan D. Hedrick (Oxford University Press, 1994), page 208.

Day Eleven: Stand Up for What's Right
1. "Sophie Scholl and the White Rose," Margie Burns, The International Raoul Wallenberg Foundation, www.raoulwallenberg.net/holocaust/articles-20/ sophie-scholl-white-rose

Day Fourteen: Forgiveness
1. "*Guideposts* Classics: Corrie Ten Boom on Forgiveness," Corrie Ten Boom, *Guideposts*, www.guideposts.org/ better-living/positive-living/guideposts-classics-corrie -ten-boom-on-forgiveness

Day Fifteen: Overcome Obstacles
1. *Wilma: The Story of Wilma Rudolph*, Wilma Rudolph (Signet, 1977).

Day Nineteen: Enduring Service
1. *Mother Teresa: A Complete Authorized Biography*, Kathryn Spink (HarperCollins, 1997), page 37.

2. "Top 20 Most Inspiring Mother Teresa Quotes," Goalcast, www.goalcast.com/2017/04/10/top-20-most-inspiring-mother-teresa-quotes

Day Twenty-Six: Face Conflict

1. *Reflections by Rosa Parks: The Quiet Strength and Faith of a Woman Who Changed a Nation*, Rosa Parks with Gregory J. Reed (Zondervan, 2017), page 22.

Day Twenty-Nine: Speak Up for Others

1. *Sojourner Truth: A Life, A Symbol*, Nell Irvin Painter (W.W. Norton & Co Inc, 1996), introduction.

Day Thirty: Defy the Norm

1. "Jesus was Her Guru," Keith J. White, Christian History Institute, www.christianhistoryinstitute.org/magazine/article/jesus-was-her-guru

Day Thirty-Four: Rescue Others

1. *The Moses of Her People*, Sarah Bradford (Geo. R. Lockwood & Son, 1886), page 29.

2. Quote originally recorded in *Scenes in the Life of Harriet Tubman*, Sarah Hopkins (W.J. Moses, Printer, 1869), page 19; spelling has been updated to match current usage.

Day Thirty-Six: Brave Humility

1. "From the Archives—Betty Cuthbert," Peter Hallett, *Sports Spectrum*, www.sportsspectrum.com/featured -article-homepage/2012/07/12/from-the-archives-betty -cuthbert

2. "Betty Cuthbert, Australia's 'Golden Girl' of Track and Field, Dies at 79," Richard Goldstein, *New York Times*, www.nytimes.com/2017/08/06/sports/olympics/betty -cuthbert-dead-australian-olympic-sprinter.html

Day Thirty-Seven: Confident Purpose

1. *The Life of Catherine Booth: The Mother of the Salvation Army, Volume 2*, Frederick St. George De Lautour Booth-Tucker (Fleming H. Revell Company, 1892), page 411.

Day Thirty-Nine: Power of Compassion

1. "Remembering An 'Angel,'" Steve Rempe, Prison Fellowship, www.prisonfellowship.org/2016/04/ remembering-an-angel

Day Forty-One: Christ in Everyone

1. *Loaves and Fishes*, Dorothy Day (Orbis Books, 1997), page 13.

2. "Servant of God Dorothy Day," Jim Forest; from text originally written for *The Encyclopedia of American Catholic History* (Liturgical Press), accessed via updated text in article posted on The Catholic

Worker Movement website, www.catholicworker.org/
dorothyday/servant-of-god.html

3. From *The Long Loneliness*, Dorothy Day (HarperCollins
reprint edition, 2017).

Day Forty-Nine: God-Given Desires

1. *The Gold Cord: The Story of a Fellowship*, Amy
Carmichael (CLC Publications, 2002), page 15.

Day Fifty: Called to the Extraordinary

1. *And It Was Good: Reflections on Beginnings*, Madeleine
L'Engle (Convergent Books, 2017), page 105.

Day Fifty-One: Keep Your Focus

1. *Fanny Crosby: Safe in the Arms of Jesus*, Chester Hearn
and S. Ann Hearn (CLC Publications, 2011).

Day Fifty-Seven: Lifelong Learners

1. *I Believe . . .: The Eighteenth Arthur Stanley Eddington
Memorial Lecture, 6 November 1964*, Kathleen
Lonsdale (Cambridge University Press, 1964), page 55.

Adored

365 Devotions for Young Women

From bullying and social media to friendships and dating, *Adored: 365 Devotions for Young Women* tackles the toughest topics girls ages 13 and up face, giving you the truth and guidance you need to face each day with confidence and grace.

Expectations and pressure. How you dress and who you date. It's tougher than ever to be a young woman who stays true to herself these days. *Adored* can help.

Adored is a daily devotional that will help you focus on what's *truly* important, so that you can live your life in the freedom of knowing you are infinitely precious in God's sight. Each day features an easy-to-read, relevant devotion, a Scripture verse, and journaling space to help you reflect on the day's message.

With honest, relatable, and sometimes humorous text, every page speaks to the pressures and changes young women face. Ultimately, *Adored* gives you real-world ways to find God in your heart, and firm ground in an ever-changing world, so that you are never caged to the latest status update, fashion trend, or crush.

Adored: 365 Devotions for Young Women:

Is a daily devotional designed for everyday use—sometimes it will give you just the right inspiration to start or end your day; other times it will be like your life raft on those *really* bad days

Will resonate with girls ages 13 and up who are searching for truth and guidance

Is the perfect gift for birthdays and high school and college graduations

Features a beautiful foiled cover

Available now wherever books are sold!

Beloved

365 Devotions for Young Women

Beloved: 365 Devotions for Young Women is an honest, poignant, sometimes humorous daily devotional that speaks to the pressures and changes girls face, giving them real-world applications to find God in their hearts and in their lives.

Using inspiring stories of girls and women in the Bible—such as Ruth, Esther, Abigail, and Mary—*Beloved: 365 Devotions for Young Women* is a topical devotional that encourages faith and confidence in girls ages 13 and up.

Each day features an easy-to-read, relevant devotion paired with a scripture verse about a biblical girl or woman, as well as journaling space to help you reflect on the day's message. Perfect for everyday use, *Beloved* will resonate with anyone searching for truth and guidance, providing insight into topics like relationships, inner beauty, and chasing your dreams.

Beloved: 365 Devotions for Young Women:

Touches on important topics in a young woman's life, such as self-esteem, self-worth, body image, gender, sexuality, friendships, dating, confidence, and much more

Includes journaling space for young women to write their thoughts, questions, and reflections

Features a beautiful foiled cover

Includes a ribbon marker

Available now wherever books are sold!